Ann, Bob and Nessie on a Sunday school trip

ALIAS CHARLIE

The autobiography of
Bob Stirling

A SQUARE ONE PUBLICATION

First published in 2000 by
Square One Publications
The Tudor House, 16 Church Street,
Upton on Severn, Worcestershire WR8 0HT

© R Stirling, 2000

ISBN: 1 89995 42 9

British Library Cataloguing in Publication Data is available
for this book

Typeset by Avon Dataset Ltd, Bidford on Avon B50 4JH

Printed in Great Britain by Biddles Ltd, Guildford, England

Acknowledgements

My sincere thanks to my daughter-in-law Vera, who managed to translate my scrawl into a manuscript on her computer; and to Mary Wilkinson for her helpful advice

Chapter 1

LOFTY

Chance is a strange thing. If Charlie Greene hadn't failed his Italian exam at university his future life would have been very different. To get his M A degree he needed to pass a foreign language. Since he wasn't very good at French and Italian was supposed to be easy he chose to try Italian. Unfortunately, what he learned was mainly Italian history. The great heroes were Garibaldi and Mussolini; Garibaldi united the different states to become Italy and Mussolini had drained the Pontine Marshes thus ridding Rome of malaria. Of the language he learned very little. The upshot was, he would need to go back to University for part of the following year.

Fortune changed for him when the Military Training Act 1939 was passed. Neville Chamberlain had come back from Munich waving a piece of paper and saying, "Peace In Our Time". However, politicians don't always mean what they say and a rush started to increase the size of the armed forces and speed up rearmament. The Act introduced conscription in peace time. Young men of twenty were to be called up to serve in the forces for six months.

Charlie arranged to be called up with the first batch of militiamen on July 14th 1939. He, with 1200 others from all over Scotland arrived at Stobs Camp near Hawick. They were in the main young, non-smoking, innocent virgins and teetotallers. Charlie found difficulty in trying to understand the dialects spoken by some of the others, particularly those from Dundee.

At Stobs Camp they were put into squads under the charge of

1

Stobs Camp

Gunner Stirling

regular army corporals. They slept on palliasses filled with straw resting on the bare floor. It was all pretty primitive but Charlie relished all the physical activities, the marching, rifle drill, weapon training and so on. It was all so different from the years of study. Charlie's squad soon became a unit. Many were given nicknames and Charlie became Lofty. When he had been in the Boys' Brigade he'd learned how to march and had become right marker. Inevitably, he became right marker for the squad. The corporal would shout, "Right Marker" and Charlie would march out and stand in front facing the corporal who would then shout, "Squad fall in". The others would then line up to the left of Lofty.

Lofty played in the squad football team and swam in the open air pool through which a river flowed. There was no problem getting off to sleep at night.

However, there was one problem that began to bug the squaddies. The food wasn't to their liking. It was different to what they were used to at home and there seemed to be a shortage of meat. Each day the orderly officer and sergeant came into the dining hall. The sergeant would shout out, "Any complaints". Although there were plenty nobody felt able to voice them. Lofty was deputed by his table to make the complaints. Each day there was always something and Lofty would stand up to say what was wrong. After a few weeks all the officers had got to know Lofty. Incidentally, much later on, the catering officer decided to have a check made on this particular cookhouse. Lofty's complaints had been relayed back to him by the other officers. The result of the investigation was that the cook and local butcher were working a fiddle. The butcher was found to be supplying only half the meat the cook had been signing for.

Although the militiamen were in the Army they were still to be regarded as civilians. Men came from Burtons, the tailors, to measure them for walking out dress. This consisted of a black blazer, black beret, black tie, khaki shirt and grey flannel trousers.

On Saturday mornings they usually went for a ten mile route march. After dinner they would change into their walking out clothes. One afternoon Lofty and hundreds of others went to the pictures. When Lofty woke up he found all around him were fast asleep. Nobody had seen the film.

On Sunday the 3rd September the battery was paraded on the square to be told that Britain was now at war with Germany.

One afternoon, two weeks later, Lofty was doing P.E. when he was summoned to go immediately to the battery office. When he got there he tried to find out why he had been sent for. The clerk in the office thought there was a job going in the quartermaster's store and the job would carry a lance corporal's stripe. When Lofty saw the major he was asked a few questions then told to change into his best uniform and report to the adjutant at 4p.m. When he got there, there were three others. After his interview the adjutant told him to report to the Colonel at 10a.m. the following morning. One of the others had been dropped and now there was just three of them. The other two had gone to fee paying schools and had been in the Officers' Training Corps. Lofty had been a pupil at an ordinary state secondary school which had no O.T.C. When he was interviewed by the Colonel he was asked why he hadn't joined the O.T.C. when he was at University. Lofty said he'd been a pacifist. The Colonel wanted to know what had caused him to change his mind. Lofty said, "The way the Germans are treating the Jews". This answer seemed to please the Colonel who then went on to detail all the wrongs being committed by the Germans. Lofty agreed. Then the Colonel said, "I am sending you to the Officers' Training Unit at Shrivenham for training to become an officer in the Royal Artillery".

A new life had started for Charlie, a big venture into the unknown.

P.S. A year later Charlie was awarded a war degree based on the subjects he had already passed. He never did pass Italian.

Chapter 2

Charlie Greene was born in 1919 the only son and the eldest child of a family of three. His father, Thomas, worked in the Clydebank shipyard earning good money with plenty of overtime during the war. His mother before her marriage had worked on the tramcars as a conductress. The family lived in a room and kitchen flat, which had a lobby and an indoor bathroom with toilet, as part of the tenement which was owned by John Brown's shipyard. Charlies's paternal grandparents lived nearby in houses occupied by foremen in the yard. His maternal grandmother was a widow who lived in Possilpark which was two tramcar rides away. It was a long journey for the young children but each Saturday they would go and enjoy themselves. Living with his grandmother were Nessie her daughter and Willie her son and Will her brother. The family were relatively poor but the humour was endless. Charlie's mother Marion would start laughing shortly after they arrived and the tears of laughter would keep running most of the afternoon and early evening.

Charlie's paternal grandparents, Old Bob and Old Bella were more Calvanistic in their attitude. Marion and Tommy would go there one evening a week. On weekdays they played 'Newmarket' with playing cards for small money stakes but if they went on a Sunday it had to be dominoes with no gambling.

Clearly Charlie had a good family life. Being the sole boy he was not allowed to do any housework. He never had to wash or dry up after a meal. He wasn't allowed to clean his own shoes or boots. All this meant that he was particularly handicapped when he was called up for the militia. Bed making, polishing and so on was more difficult to do than it might otherwise have been. When he was about five he started to run errands for his grandmother to the local Co-op shops. She was very explicit about what she wanted. When he went to the butcher's to buy mince he was instructed to ask for a pound of the best steak. When this had been cut he then had to ask the butcher to mince it.

Charlie started school when he was five and his father started teaching him the multiplication tables. This together with granny's shopping developed his ability to do mental arithmetic at a level beyond that of his classmates. It was decided, by the school, that he should be promoted a year but even then his mental arithmetic was way ahead of his new classmates.

At the age of seven the local education authority decided to alter the catchment areas for the local schools and Charlie and others were sent to a school much nearer home. For some reason Charlie was moved up another year so he was now two years younger than his classmates. They had been taught how to do handwriting. Charlied could only do printing. His attempts at writing and drawing were pathetic, so much so that when his mother visited his class on an open afternoon, she asked the teacher why none of Charlie's work was on display, only to be told that, "It wouldn't be fair to Charlie to display his work on the wall."

To go on to secondary school the children had to sit a qualifying exam at the age of 12. Charlie actually sat the exam while he was still only nine. As part of the English exam there was a piece of dictation. The headteacher read out a piece from the editorial of the day's Glasgow Herald. It was a difficult piece for a young pupil to understand and some of the words were very hard to spell. The arithmetic exam. started off with questions so simple that Charlie felt he must be doing something wrong. Only when he got onto the harder questions and problems did he feel comfortable.

Clydebank High School was a co-educational comprehensive school for all the pupils in the catchment area. For the purpose of teaching, each year was divided into streams. The top stream contained a boys' class and a girls' class. This was called the 'Professional Group'. These pupils were taught Latin and French.

The next group was 'Technical or Commercial. The boys were Technical, the girls Commercial. These groups were taught French.

ALIAS CHARLIE

The third stream was the 'Practical Group', where no foreign language was taught and where the main emphasis was on practical subjects, woodwork for boys, cooking and sewing for girls. There was also a a remedial group at the bottom of the school where the emphasis was on reading and simple sums.

Charlie was placed in the Technical stream. He was a day dreamer. Apart from mathematics he showed no promise. He did no homework at home. When he got to school in the morning he would ask his classmates what homework had been set, then he would scribble something in his jotters to show that he had made some attempt.

At the end of the second year, his teachers thought that he had been advanced too far so he repeated the second year. He had been top in Maths but low in most other subjects.

In the repeated second year he began to learn some French. His new teacher Jimmie Logie gave them a spelling test each Friday. For every mistake that was made, a pupil would get hit on the hand with his leather strap. There's no doubt that this was a very effective means of teaching.

Most of the pupils in the school left at the end of the second year when they were 14. Charlie was still too young to leave so proceeded into the third year. At the end of this year there was the Scottish Leaving Certificate exams. By then Charlie was beginning to show some ability in Science as well as Maths. After the written exams there were oral or practical exams conducted by school inspectors. The pupils who were in the Professional Group by-passed these exams for they were aiming for the Higher Certificate exams at the end of the fifth year.

Charlie had been given the top rating by his science teacher. This meant he was given the most difficult practical test. This was to reduce copper oxide to copper by making hydrogen then passing it through a combustion tube containing the copper oxide which was being heated by a bunsen burner, the surplus hydrogen being burned at the end of the tube. That a school inspector should expect a 13 year old pupil to carry out such an experiment is almost unbelievable. When Charlie did become a science teacher many years later, such an experiment was not performed by teachers because it was considered too dangerous.

As most of the pupils in Charlie's class were going to leave that year there was a certain amount of fooling around. This happened particularly in French lessons. They started off with a lady teacher, Fanny Galloway, who soon became ill. She was replaced by a temporary woman teacher who lasted a short while. Then another took over and so it went on. All the good work done by Jimmie Logie was undone. During one lesson the desks kept moving slowly forward until at the end of the lesson the teacher couldn't get out. It was a very cruel way to treat a teacher but the lads were just having fun.

Towards the end of the year when Charlie became 14 he was offered two jobs. One job was in the drawing office at the shipyard, the other was as a laboratory assistant at a new cement factory that was opening in Clydebank. Both jobs offered prospects for the future. Charlie's father and Charlie went round to see Old Bob to see what he thought. Old Bob felt that the cement factory might affect Charlie's chest and the job in the shipyard wasn't too attractive because of the hard time shipbuilding was having. The decision was taken that Charlie should carry on at school.

Chapter 3

Six year old Charlie was dawdling home from school when he was set upon by two eight year old lads.

"What are you, Protestant or Catholic?"

"I don't know."

"What school do you go to?"

"Elgin Street."

"Let him go, he's Protestant."

If he'd gone to the Catholic school they would have duffed him up.

When Charlie got home he asked his mum.

"What are we, Protestant or Catholic?"

"Why do you ask?"

"Two big boys grabbed hold of me and asked me."

"What happened?"

"They asked me what school I went to. When I said Elgin Street they let me go."

"Keep away from such boys. It doesn't matter whether you are a Catholic or a Protestant."

Only later in life did Charlie learn that his mother had been brought up as a Catholic and his father a Protestant.

The antagonism of some bigots was exemplified when the Orangemen went marching through the main street passing the Catholic church. Rangers and Celtic supporters get into a fever when the two teams meet. The worst occasion happened when in a match at Celtic Park the Celtic goalkeeper, John Thompson, dived on to the ball at the feet of Sammy English, the Rangers centre forward. Thompson got a boot in the head from which he died. Who was to blame was never quite clear. Did Thompson do something desperate or did English boot his head without due care? Thompson was buried, a huge crowd lining the streets.

Sammy English never kicked another ball.

Charlie was never really aware of this bigotry. The Catholics and Protestants living in his street seemed to get on well enough. There was no friction and they all joined in the street football matches. There was always a match going on in the street or in one of the fields nearby. The two main employers in the town were John Brown's Shipyard and Singer Sewing Machine factory. If you wanted to join in on a game in progress you had to have a partner also wanting to play. You'd be asked, "Singers or Brown's?" Depending on your answer you would join one team and your partner the other.

There were a large number of churches considering the size of the town and Charlie found himself involved with many of them during his childhood and adolescence. He went to Sunday School run by the Union Kirk. On Friday evenings he went to the 'Band of Hope' at the Parish Church. At the 'Band of Hope' they were warned of the dangers of alcohol and took the pledge to refrain from drinking alcohol. He joined the cubs at the Episcopal Church, (the Church of England). During the depression he went to the Baptist Church on a Saturday evening when there would be a concert, a cup of tea and a bag of buns. On a Sunday morning he would go to Hamilton Memorial Church with his mother, grandfather and sisters. His grandfather, 'Old Bob', was hard of hearing and headphones were installed at his place at the end of the pew. He would put them on to hear the sermon but Charlie, who sat beside him, had always to find the hymn for him in the hymn book.

When Charlie was about ten he left the cubs and went to join the Boys' Brigade. About this age he also joined the Clydebank Junior Male Voice Choir. He really enjoyed going along on a Thursday evening to sing with the choir. On a cold winter's evening they would leave the hall feeling really high then pop into the fish and chip shop for a packet of chips wrapped in newspaper. The choir sang at festivals and gave concerts, establishing a very good reputation.

At Sunday School, Charlie was always very attentive and each year at the Christmas Concert he would be awarded a book inscribed for excellence. During this period he wanted to be a missionary like David Livingstone. At junior school he had a lady teacher who taught them all about the Labour Party. Each night when Charlie said his prayers he would ask God to bless all the members of his family and ask God to bless the Labour Party.

Sometimes when he said 'For ever and ever, Amen', he tried to visualise what for ever and ever meant. Did it mean a million years, a million, million years or more that that? He would become so disturbed that he'd get out of bed and go into the kitchen for a drink of water to get the matter out of his head.

Charlie was never lonely as a child. There were lots of children in the street. There was always some activity going on, football, cricket, conkers, marbles, games with cigarette cards, hop scotch, skipping and many others. It was a closely knit community and if you did anything wrong your parents would soon get to know and you would have to answer to them.

Chapter 4

During the First World War there was a big demand for naval ships and John Brown's Shipyard was fully utilised. After the war there was a demand for merchant ships which lasted only a few years. In the late nineteen twenties the outlook was bleak, then on 1st December, 1930 the Cunard Shipping Company placed an order to build the largest passenger liner in the world to be used on the transatlantic route. Work proceeded apace and soon the giant hull began to dominate the town.

However, the world economy slipped into financial crisis in the second half of 1931 and on 12th December, 1931, Cunard was forced to suspend financial support for the building of the vessel.

Charlie remembers that day very clearly. The men came out of the yard at the end of the shift thinking they were going to have an extended Christmas holiday. Little did they realise what the next two and a half years would bring. A few men, mainly foremen, were kept on to do maintenance on the equipment. The ship was painted with red lead paint to prevent it rusting away.

There was no work to be obtained in the other shipyards and the giant Singer Sewing Machine factory was suffering too. The problem was not confined to Clydeside. It was world wide.

In Clydebank most adults were out of work. At first shopkeepers were willing to give customers goods on credit. It soon became apparent that they wouldn't be paid and the shops started to go into bankruptcy. The town became a depressing place. At every street corner there were groups just standing with nothing to do. Many shops had closed. The rents on houses were not being paid. There began a series of moonlight flits. Landlords would give notice to tenants to pay up or be forced out of their houses. At night a handcart would appear to carry all the material belongings of the family to another house which they'd managed to rent.

12

ALIAS CHARLIE

John Brown's yard bought a large field which they fenced in and let off to some of their unemployed to form allotments. Charlie's father got one. They were given seeds at a very low price and soon the whole area was in cultivation. Every plot had its own manure heap. Much transport was still horse drawn and there were always 'plotters' ready to scoop up the horse manure from the streets. A vacancy occurred for a roadsweeper. Two hundred and fifty men applied for the post and there was great annoyance when a councillor's son got the job.

The government introduced the 'Means Test'. After you had been on the dole for a few months you were means tested. If you had savings, the dole money was reduced until all your savings had gone. If one member of a family was working his earnings were taken into account when supplying dole money to others. Men were forced to leave family homes to live somewhere else so that they could continue to receive the unemployment money.

Charlie's family was a little better off than most. Old Bob being a head foreman kept on working at the yard. He gave 5/- a week to each of his unemployed sons. Since the dole money for Charlie's family was 29/- a week, this 5/- was a great help.

Charlie's father was unemployed for about a year and a half, then he was re-employed to help build a naval ship which had been ordered.

Now that his father was off the dole Charlie was able to take on a morning job at the local Coop. dairy. At 6.00a.m. the milk boys filled their barrows with bottles of milk which they delivered to various houses on their round. Charlie had about 75 houses to serve. The job occupied about two hours daily so that he was back home at eight in time to have breakfast before setting off to school. For the seven mornings work he received 4/6d. Later the pay was increased to 6/-.

The period of hardship in his youth made an indelible impression on Charlie. Apart from his mortgage he never borrowed a penny from anywhere. If he couldn't pay for an article he went without.

Work restarted on the liner 534 on 3rd April, 1934 and on the 26th September, Queen Mary accompanied by King George V, launched the ship and named it the Queen Mary. Thousands of people came to watch the launching. On the opposite side of the river, a small river, the River Cart was supposed to receive the displaced water as the ship entered the Clyde. Rows of seating had been erected on the other bank for the spectators who were unconnected with the yard and therefore didn't receive invitations. The huge ship started to slide down the slipway and the massive chain links required to stop her when she had entered the water started to snap. A huge tidal wave swept over the spectators on the far bank. After the launch the ship went into the fitting out basin. In 1936 the ship set sail down the Clyde being towed by powerful tugs and others who kept her in position. The townspeople had a day's holiday and crowds watched as the beautiful ship left Clydebank. Before the sail down the Clyde the families of the workers were invited to look round the ship. It was beautiful and Charlie was thrilled to think that so many of the men he knew had contributed so much to create it. He realised that he was living amongst a group of craftsmen so varied and gifted the like of which existed nowhere else in the world.

During the thirties, two Japanese men spent time at the yard learning how to build ships. The feeling was that the Japs would never be able to build ships like Clydebank. Pearl Harbour was to give the lie to this thought.

Chapter 5

Charlie stayed on at school. He was still the youngest pupil in the year. There were about fifty pupils in the year, almost all from the two professional streams. The target was to prepare for the Scottish Higher Leaving Certificate at the end of the 5th year. The exams for this certificate could be taken at either a higher or lower level. Since Charlie had come from a lower stream he was targeted towards the lower levels. During the 4th year, Miss Lowe, the senior mistress taught them about arithmetic progression. She said that she would test the pupils in the next lesson and that they were to revise the work from the textbook. After the test Miss Lowe asked Charlie to stay behind. She asked, "Did you revise as I told you?"

"Yes Miss Lowe", said Charlie.

"How did you manage to do that when you left your textbook in the classroom?"

Charlie had to confess that he hadn't revised. Unkown to him, he was the only pupil in the class to get it all right.

Miss Lowe had a discussion with Jock Lindsay, the head of department, and as a result Charlie was moved up into the top set. The subjects Charlie was studying were maths., English, science and French.

The maths, involved Euclidean geometry, algebra, trigonometry, arithmetic and analytical geometry. To pass in science you had to pass in physics and chemistry. English consisted of three exams., language, literature and history. French had a paper on language and on literature with an oral exam. History was a subject Charlie had always enjoyed. The battles against the English, Bannockburn, Flodden and the rest. The story of the Covenanters and of Jenny Geddes declaiming against the prayer book in St. Giles Cathedral fired his interest. These, with the annual football and rugby matches against England were the stuff of life. For the higher history exam the study was mainly based on the Agrarian and Industrial Revolution.

The English literature section was very demanding. Over the years they had studied five Shakespeare plays, The Merchant of Venice, Julius Caesar, The Tempest, Macbeth and finally Hamlet. They had read extensively works by Sir Walter Scott, Robert Burns, Robert Louis Stevenson, John Buchan and others. They had studied Palgraves' Golden Treasury of Poems, Chaucer's prologue to the Canterbury Tales, Milton's Paradise Lost , Paradise Regained, l'Allegro and Il Penseroso, Alexander Pope's Rape of the Lock and many more.

Passages of prose and poetry had to be learned by heart so that they could be quoted. The literature and history papers were demanding as well as the language paper which required a long essay and a firm knowledge of English grammar.

Midway during the 5th year school exams were taken to decide finally which standard of exam was to be attempted. English had to be taken at the higher level. French for Charlie was at the lower level. Maths. was higher. In the science exams Charlie did particularly well. He was top of the year in Physics and well up in Chemistry. As a result he was promoted into the top science groups.

In the higher exams he passed English and science but failed maths. and lower French. The failure in maths was a big shock to Charlie and his teacher. Charlie had not properly revised the theorems in Euclidean geometry and he failed on this.

The end result was that Charlie would need to repeat the 5th year. Although he had passed English he had to sit that exam again as well as maths. and French. This time he was amongst his peer group and managed to pass the exams quite easily. The day of the Maths exam was the day the Queen Mary sailed down the Clyde. The town and the school had a public holiday to watch the spectacle. Because the exams had to be taken at the same time as the rest of the schools in Scotland, about thirty pupils assembled in the school hall to take the exam. Charlie did all the morning paper checked it through quickly then went to hand it in to Miss

ALIAS CHARLIE

Lowe who was the invigilator. She was reluctant to take the paper from him but he persuaded her that he had done it all and checked that it was all done right.

He dashed out of the hall, ran up the stairs of the main building then up to the roof where the school janitor was watching. Charlie saw the Queen Mary as it approached a bend in the river before going out of sight. He was the only examinee who saw it.

He learned much later that he had not got it all right. He got 92% for the morning exam and 96% for the afternoon paper. A mark which the school inspector said was one of the best in the West of Scotland.

Clydebank High School did well for Charlie and his peers. It was perhaps unfortunate that he had been advanced those two extra years in primary school. He might have gone into the Professional class then. However it seemed to work out all right in the end.

Charlie played for the school cricket team and rugby team. For two years he was secretary for the cricket team and helped to arrange matches against other schools. He had the keys to the sports field pavilion. In the winter a group would go up to the playing field and practise rugby. In the summer it would be cricket. He and a few others prepared the wicket for the matches. Needless to say even though they rolled it plenty, it tended to be bumpy making batting quite difficult.

Miss Lowe used to hold ballroom dancing sessions to prepare for the annual dance. She made sure that all the girls got partners for each dance. Charlie enjoyed taking part in the various dances such as the Eightsome Reel, Valetta, St. Bernard's Waltz, Gay Gordons and so on. Although he was never a good dancer he had enough confidence to go onto the floor in his university and army days.

The next period of his life was to be the three years at Glasgow University.

Chapter 6

Charlie had a great friend, John Kinloch, who was a year older. They did so many things together. They were milk boys, played in the school teams and were near neighbours. On the first day at University, Charlie and John went up by bus. Charlie's first lecture was at 9 a.m. The subject was 'Natural Philosophy' which we now call Physics. The professor always took this lesson which was held in a large tiered lecture theatre. The seating arrangement was that the girls sat in the front rows and the lads at the back. Unknown to Charlie many of the lads from the previous year turned up to stand at the back. John told Charlie to go in at the lower entrance while he was going up the back entrance. When Charlie came in by this entrance, which was the one for girls, there was a great shout. Blushing badly, Charlie had to climb up the steps to the area where lads sat.

Sitting at the demonstration bench was the chief lab technician, a highlander of about forty who was called Duncan. It was at the time that knock, knock jokes were popular. Someone got up and shouted, "Knock, knock", to be answered by, "Who goes there"? "Duncan", "Duncan who"?, "Dung can make the grass grow".

When the professor entered the theatre there was a great cheer from the back. Then they began to sing, "Professor Jones we love you well. Do we hell, do we hell. Professor Jones we wish you luck. Do we hell, do we well". John Kinloch was leading the singing and the Professor summoned him to come down to the front to be admonished in a joking sort of way. This was Charlie's introduction to studies at the University.

He had enrolled for a four year MA honours course. His main subjects being Maths and Physics. In the first year he had to take one extra Arts subject and he chose to do European History.

He passed his first year exams but not as well as he'd hoped.

ALIAS CHARLIE

Two reasons, perhaps, were the cause. First was money. It was a strain on the family resources to keep Charlie at University. Scottish students got a grant from the Andrew Carnegie Foundation which helped to pay most of the fees, but Charlie had little money to buy textbooks and usually had to try and borrow them from the library. The second reason, perhaps, was that Charlie found intensive study to be very tiring. It was another thirty years before he learned that he had astigmatism, which put a strain on his eyes when reading.

The second year's study was Maths, Physics and a Philosophy. The choice was between Moral Philosophy and Logic and Metaphysics. Charlie chose to do the latter which fitted into his timetable better.

The Logic part was involved in logical thinking as exemplified in Syllogisms such as "If A is a member of B and B is a member of C, then A is a member of C". The examples were not usually as simple as that.

The Philosophy part dealt with the works of some of the great philosophers, Socrates, Plato, Aristotle, Descartes, Kant, Locke, Hume, Russell and other recent philosophers.

It was known to be a very hard subject and Charlie failed his first attempt and had to resit it. Although he passed in Maths and Natural Philosophy he didn't have the high marks that would lead to a high honours degree. He decided to aim for the Ordinary degree. Here he came upon a problem. If he'd started on a B.Sc. degree he could study more sciences but an ordinary M.A. required the study of a foreign language. The year of fooling around in school had meant that he had not been able to do his Highers in French. It was unlikely that he would be able to cope with it at University level. He was told that Italian was a much easier subject, so he chose that.

Life at University was not all hard slog. True he had to stay in, in the evenings when other friends were able to go out. He rarely got time to go out on Sunday evenings on the 'Monkey Walk'. This was a process where boys walked along a route round a public park and girls walked along the same route in the opposite direction. The distance involved was about two to three miles.

19

The lads would try to chat up the girls, sometimes successfully. There was no hanky panky going on but it allowed various groups a chance to get to know each other.

In his first year Charlie joined the Physical Society. This society met regularly to hear talks from various people. The Natural Philosophy department was housed in a building full of mementos of Lord Kelvin who had for many years been the professor. Some of the talks were given by post graduate students but occasionally some famous scientist would come. Charlie remembers the talk by CTR Wilson the inventor of the Cloud Chamber, a process by which the particles from an atom made a trail through a tube which had most of the air taken out. These particles left a flight pattern just like an aircraft does when flying high in the sky. Another famous visitor was Max Planck, who explained how light could be explained as a wave pattern and also as a series of particles striking an object. Planck's Constant was one of the discoveries leading up to the splitting of the atom.

Some times the society would go to factories or works to see what went on. One visit Charlie remembers vividly was a visit to a coal mine. They were all told to wear old clothes. They went down the mine shaft very quickly, then proceeded along the mine to the coal face where the coal was being cut and loaded on to a conveyor belt.

At the end of the visit their hair, eyes, nose and clothes were thick with coal dust. There were no facilities for washing so they had to return to their homes covered in grime.

On his first visit, Charlie was approached by a committee member to see if he was willing to represent the first year lads on the committee. A girl was also invited on to the committee. His selection didn't please one male who wanted to know why Charlie was selected. He was an outstanding scholar who went on to become a professor of mathematics. In the second year Charlie became librarian and the embryo professor was elected to the committee.

University pupils used to have a 'Rag Week' where they would do things to get money for charity. They used to dress up in fancy clothes and go with collection tins to collect money. Dressed as they were they would go anywhere.

Shortly after the birth of the Dionne quins in Canada, the students of Clydebank announced in the local press that a lady had given birth to sextuplets. The name of the family and their location was being kept secret for the moment. Many people took this news seriously and the story got world wide credence, even appearing in the column of a South African paper.

The following week it was reported that the sextuplets, their mother Ma Gowk (April Fool) and doctor, Doctor Latrine would appear at a concert being given by the students on the Friday evening before Rag Saturday. Charlie was chosen to be the one female. On the Friday evening they went along to the railway station at Yoker where they put on their baby clothes in the waiting room. They then went by train to the Clydebank Central Station which was a terminus two miles away. There they were met by a group of students pulling a cleaned up dustcart being used as a pram. They were pulled along the road to the Town Hall where they were presented to the Provost and a large audience who had come to the concert.

One Rag Day, John Kinloch and Charlie decided to go to Ayr to take part in their Rag Day. John's mother made two thin blouses for them and they borrowed gym slips which since they were both over six feet barely covered their bottoms. The day started off well enough but as the breeze from the sea got stronger and colder they realised they were inadequately clothed so they slipped into the cinema and sat there to keep warm until it was time to go back in the bus.

The four Scottish universities, Glasgow, Edinburgh, St. Andrews and Aberdeen had a tradition whereby students elected a rector to represent them. In 1937 the candidates included Winston Churchill (Winnie the Pooh) and Canon Dick Sheppard a well known pacifist. The election took place starting at 10 a.m. on a Saturday morning. Students would dress up in rugby clothes and carry bags of soot or flour to throw at the opposing supporters. Each group made an effort to keep the opposing parties out of the hall where polling took place. After the initial skirmishing people went in to record their votes. Dick Sheppard was elected by a large margin. They were all pacifists in those days. They didn't realise what was going to happen in the years ahead.

Chapter 7

Towards the end of September 1939, Charlie, Jake and Paul left Stobs Camp to go to Shrivenham. It was a long train journey but it was exciting to be going to somewhere new.

The military college at Shrivenham consisted of two very large buildings, each with their own parade ground. One building was used for training with anti-aircraft weapons. The other was for searchlights. The three of them went to the searchlight training camp.

When they got there the buildings were not yet finished. The toilets were outside in a large hut. Two long rows of toilets made evacuation a communal experience.

The first intake of cadets came from three sources. Some, like Charlie, had come from the various militia camps throughout the country. About a third of the cadets were older people who had been in the OTC. The third group were cadets from the regular army Royal Artillery College at Woolwich, which was known as 'The Shop'.

The three lads from Stobs Camp found themselves at a slight disadvantage. They had been given First World War uniforms. The jackets had 1917 stamped inside. The trousers were old cavalry type jodhpurs. These fastened just below the knee. Below that, puttees were worn. These were long rolls of khaki cloth about four inches thick. They were would round each leg. If they were wound too tight, circulation of blood was hindered. If wound too loose, they would start to slip down the legs. Getting dressed quickly was a problem and as everything was done at the double and all the other cadets had the new battledress with long trousers it meant that the three lads were always last to arrive at the lesson following P T.

The officers at the college were a mixed bunch. Some were

regular officers in the Royal Artillery but many were from the reserve army. Some of these had risen through the ranks in the First World War. One who was particularly helpful to Charlie was a Cockney, rumoured to have been a nightwatchman on the site before being called up again as a captain.

As cadets they were expected to drill better than other ranks. One cadet, a barrister in civilian life, was unable to march properly. He was inclined to do the 'donkey walk', the walk where the left arm and left leg would go forward at the same time. It was decided that he was not cut out to be an army officer so he was returned to civilian life.

At the end of October they were given a 36 hour leave. Charlie decided to go home. He travelled from Swindon, to London and from there by another train to Glasgow. He arrived home at tea time. After tea, some friends called to see him but Charlie had fallen asleep in an armchair and didn't wake up till bedtime when he went to bed. He then had to catch his bus to Glasgow, first thing in the morning and arrived back at Shrivenham late on the same evening.

The next time they had a 36 hour leave Charlie, Jake and Paul decided to stay in London at a Caledonian Society hostel. Charlie and Paul went to Hammersmith Palais to dance to the music of Joe Loss and his orchestra. Jake wanted to see the show at the Windmill theatre, so he went on his own.

The course at Shrivenham was a bit makeshift. Most of the officers didn't know much about searchlights and it wasn't until he left Shrivenham and joined a searchlight regiment that he learned about the equipment and crew required to man the light.

One of the things Charlie had to learn was how to drive a car. He was given some driving lessons on old cars. One Saturday he went to Oxford to play rugby against one of the colleges. They went in cars and each was allowed to drive part of the way there or back. Just before the end of their training they had to take a driving test which consisted of a drive round the barrack square and reversing into a lane. They were then given driving licences which allowed them to drive anything from a motor cycle to a three ton lorry.

Towards the end of November a representative from a clothing firm arrived to measure the cadets for their officer's uniform. Everything they could possibly need was sold to them. Each cadet was allowed £35 to spend on his kit and this rep. made sure they spent it all.

Copy of uniform bill

		£	s	d
November 20th	Tunic	5	19	6
	Slacks	2	2	0
	Greatcoat	8	8	0
	Sam Browne Belt	1	10	0
	Whistle and Lanyard		3	0
	Cap	1	5	0
	Cloth Belt	—	—	—
	Shirt		12	6
December 11th	Gloves		4	9
	Socks 2/6 and 3/6		6	0
	Slacks	2	2	0
	Valise	2	10	0
	Flea Bag (sleeping)	2	5	0
	Haversack		16	6
	2 Shirts	1	11	0
	Camp Bed	3	3	0
	Washstand	1	3	6
	Total	£34	4	9

Other items bought later included a raincoat, ties and underwear. With the Sam Browne leather belt went a revolver holster and a 'frog' to carry a sword.

The night before they went home on leave a staff officer took some of them to the local pub where Charlie drank his first half pint of beer.

After the war Charlie received his written copy of his

commission. It read, "George the Sixth by the Grace of God, of Great Britain, Ireland and the British Dominions beyond the Seas, King, Defender of the Faith.

To Our Trusty and well beloved Charles Greene, Greetings. We reposing especial Trust and Confidence in your Loyalty, Courage and Good Conduct do by these Presents, Constitute and Appoint you to be an Officer in Our Land Forces, from the sixteenth day of December 1939. You are therefore carefully and diligently to discharge your Duty as such in the Rank of Second Lieutenant".

Given at Our Court of Saint James's. the Twenty Second day of December 1939 in the Third Year of Our Reign".

By His Majesty's Command.

Chapter 8

On the 1st of January 1940, Charlie and two others from Shrivenham were posted to a searchlight regiment with headquarters on an aerodrome at Catterick. There they met the colonel, adjutant and some other officers. The regiment had been a territorial army unit based in Sunderland. They spent two nights at Catterick before being sent to the three batteries, one at Ripon, one at Stokesley and the third at Thirsk. Charlie went to Thirsk. Whilst they were at Catterick they were shown a new secret defence weapon which was able to detect enemy aircraft by radio location. Radar as it is now called was in its infancy then.

At Thirsk Charlie stayed at battery HQ for about three weeks. It was a bitterly cold winter and the camp was only partly built. The officers slept in tents which were so cold that the Brylcreem Charlie used as hair dressing froze in the jar and the glass cracked. One evening his batman put a hot water bottle in his camp bed. When Charlie went to bed the hot water had turned to ice. In the morning Charlie would rise, put on his clothes and boots as best as he could. He'd go over to the mess hut where there was a stove. Here he would thaw out until he was able to fasten his buttons and tie the laces of his boots.

The battery consisted of three troops and each troop had six searchlight sites spread about three or four miles apart. One troop had its sites situated on the hills of the North Yorkshire Moors. To reach the sites the normal way was to go up Sutton Bank but there was so much snow and ice that there was no possibility of a vehicle going up that road. The daily rations and mail had to be delivered by two different round about routes. Even so the site at Cold Kirby could not be reached. Fortunately the site was near the local pub which was able to provide their food. The company commander was so worried about the situation at Cold Kirby that he went back to Sunderland to fetch his skis then went up Sutton Bank on his skis, a very slow and difficult journey. Charlie was used as a driver to take supplies in the major's car to some of these sites. There for the first time he saw the beautiful ruins of Rievaulx Abbey and the Abbey of Ampleforth College where some of the furniture had the little mouse carving showing that it had been made by Thompson the local carpenter at Kilburn.

As a newly qualified driver Charlie found negotiating bends on an icy road, very difficult. Sometimes he would skid into a heap of snow Fortunately there was very little traffic and there was always someone around who would help to dig him out.

After a few weeks the weather started to improve. Charlie was sent to join another officer at his troop HQ. Here he began to learn about life on searchlight sites. Once a week he would take the pay out to the men on the sites. The men would be lined up and as the name was called out the soldier would step forward, salute and receive his pay. All this saluting made him feel very important. It took him a while to learn that the site corporals and the troop sergeant knew a lot more then he did about some matters. When he did begin to realise this fact and give his subordinates freedom to do things their way, he became a better commander.

The officer i/c the troop went to battery HQ and Charlie was left in sole command. One site was near a railway line. Fuel was in short supply on site. The soldiers used to shout to the firemen on local trains for lumps of coal. Often the fireman would throw lumps of coal from the fire tender which all helped to keep the stove in the hut warm.

One of the farmers threatened to cut off the water supplies to one of the sites unless he was paid; Charlie in his ignorance did not realise that farmers had to pay for water and had a big argument with him. A few weeks later the payment for water problem was sorted and the farmer came with a leg of lamb for him. He said that one of his lambs had got caught up in some barbed wire and in the struggle to free itself had got badly ripped. There was nothing the farmer could do but kill it and he thought Charlie might like this leg. Charlie had a suspicion that the farmer felt he might be in trouble for killing a lamb for food and this was a way of extricating him from trouble.

One day a farmer's son found two young fox cubs. The vixen had been shot dead. He asked the people on the searchlight site if they wanted to have them as pets. They said they would have them and because the weather was still very cold they brought the two cubs into their living hut. Each day they were well fed from the cookhouse but the smell in the hut was a bit pungent. The cubs didn't seem to like the smell of the men either so they dug a hole under the hut and started to sleep there. One night was particularly cold and one of the cubs froze to death. The other cub was taken to Sunderland by one of the soldiers who reckoned it could be brought up like a dog.

When searchlight sites had been established for a long while with the same crew they tended to acquire stray cats and dogs who found that there was always a meal for them from the cookhouse. The problem arose when the sites had to be vacated and homes had to be found for the pets locally. One site had a parrot which had picked up a fair bit of strong language. The vicar offered to find it a home. Charlie always wondered how that problem was sorted out. These events took place a few years after Charlie had left Yorkshire.

On 1st May, 1940 Charlie transferred to 26th AA Battalion R.E. based at White City in London. This unit was known as the London Engineers and although they were in searchlights they were not R.A. but R.E. This was a group of territorial soldiers made up of many highly qualified sons of important families. Charlie was attached to a troop for two weeks then he received this message, "2/Lt Green will proceed to No 1 Section (Lords) forthwith to assume command". Charlie's new command was based at Lords Cricket Ground. His troop HQ was in a very posh house in St. John's Wood. There was a set of stairs leading from the garden into the cricket ground and the searchlight site was on the practice area. On an evening many famous cricketers would come to practise at the nets. Charlie's section's sites covered Buckingham Palace and the whole of the West End of London. Charlie would pop into a Lyon's Corner House for a late supper and listen to the orchestra and he would still be within his troop area.

One evening the corporal at the site on Green Park arrested a man who was asking too many questions. The man was taken to Bow Street police station. It transpired he was an M.P. whose brother was an important member of the Royal Household. In those days Charlie didn't know the word homosexual but it is likely that this man was looking for a mate.

After two weeks at Lords, Charlie was transferred to another troop whose HQ was at the Oval Cricket Ground. Here the searchlight was placed right in the middle of the playing area. Charlie's office and sleeping quarters were in the cricket pavilion. The head groundsman 'Boss' Martin made out a tennis court for the lads to play on. Incidentally his son was head groundsman at Lords. Charlie was always able to boast that he had played cricket at Lords and the Oval.

Outside the Kensington Oval were the big gasholders normally called gasometers, Charlie always wondered what would happen if a bomb scored a direct hit on one.

On 22nd May, 1940 Charlie received this message.

Subject: Posting Out – 2/Lt Greene

SECRET

2/Lt C Greene is placed under orders for service with the BEF (British Expeditionary Force) amongst the first reinforcements for Searchlight Regiments and will join Depot RA Woolwich on 28th May, 1940.

This information is secret. You may inform your near relatives but no one else.

2/Lt Greene may be sent on embarkation leave as soon as he can be spared.

Signed JP Widgery 2/Lt RE
For OC 26th (L.E.E.) AABn RE

ALIAS CHARLIE

This same John Widgery was to become Charlie's colonel in later years and went on to become Lord Chief Justice in civvy street.

The day after Charlie got home on embarkation leave he got a telegram recalling him to his unit. The evacuation of the BEF through Dunkirk was about to happen.

Chapter 9

After the evacuation of the BEF through Dunkirk the British Army was very short of the weapons needed to defend Britain from a German invasion. Herman Goering thought he could bomb Britain into submission. The Battle of Britain took place in the air. By this time Charlie had moved to a new troop HQ in Erith in Kent. The bombers came over in daytime and were met by fighter planes and anti-aircraft gunfire. High up in the sky Charlie could see vapour trails as the fighting took place. One of his sites on Hayes Common got the credit for shooting down a Dornier 17 with its Lewis Machine Gun.

On Saturday August 17th, 1940, King George VI came to inspect an anti-aircraft gun station on which Charlie had a site. After seeing the guns the King came to the searchlight where Charlie had his men lined up. A brigadier came to ask Charlie his name. Charlie ordered his men to 'Present Arms' then he was introduced to the King who shook hands with him and asked about the new sound locator which they were using. The King thought it was 'colossal'. Charlie reflected that it was only about six years since his grandfather 'Old Bob' had been introduced to King George V at the launch of the Queen Mary.

As the Battle of Britain was being won in the air the Germans started to do their bombing at night. This meant that Charlie and his men were on duty every night. One evening his troop sergeant was summoned to battery HQ to collect some Mills bombs (hand grenades). He went round the six sites leaving three bombs at each site. One group had the use of a house next to the field where the searchlight, sound locator and Lister generator were. The troop sergeant told the corporal in charge of the site that he had left three Mills bombs on the mantelpiece in the kitchen.

When the dawn arrived, the 'All Clear' sounded on the air raid sirens and the soldiers 'stood down' and went to bed, leaving three men to start things up if the sirens went again. These three went into the kitchen to make some tea. One man who was a bit older and simpler that the rest picked up a bomb and said,

"What is this?"

"It's a Mills bomb."

"How does it work?"

"You pull the pin out."

He pulled the pin out, the other two dashed out of the kitchen into the garden yelling to him to throw it away. He did. He threw it out of the window right into the path of the other two. Fortunately it takes a few seconds for the bomb to explode and they were able to get away from the main force of the blast. One got a piece of shrapnel in his backside.

Needless to say there was a court of inquiry. The sergeant was rebuked for leaving the Mills bombs on the mantelpiece. The gunner was discharged from the army as he was more of a danger than a help.

It is hard, in later years to realise how well the Londoners behaved during the War. There was this sense of comradeship and responsibility. Men, after a day's work would stay up at night to do firewatching. The Germans dropped masses of little incendiary bombs. If they were allowed to keep burning they could set a building ablaze. Firewatchers had buckets of sand and a long handled shovel. The shovel would pick up the bomb and deposit it in the bucket where it would burn out harmlessly or be covered with sand and extinguished. They also had STIRRUP pumps to put out fires with jets of water. Every flat roofed building had its firewatchers on duty on the roof. The firewatchers, Home Guard, air raid wardens, fire brigades and police all did wonderful work.

Charlie had never believed that the Anderson shelters would be any good. These were little huts made of corrugated iron which were partly buried in the ground and had earth heaped over them. One night there was a huge bang and when Charlie went to look, a house had been completely destroyed. The family who were in the Anderson shelter in the garden came out very dazed but completely unhurt.

It was also interesting to see the effect of bomb blasts on windows. On some occasions the wave of air would cause the window to go in. On other occasions the window would withstand the first wave but then collapse outwards as a trough followed the wave.

Because of the bombing it was essential that every building was blacked out. The air raid wardens checked on that. There were no street lights. Church bells were silenced. They were only to be rung as a warning of an invasion. Vehicle lights were reduced to a tiny little cross making it very difficult to see ahead. When driving at night it was safest to go slowly and drive near the middle of the road.

All road signs were removed so that invading Germans wouldn't know where to go. In the event, as no Germans invaded, the lack of road signs sometimes resulted in you getting lost.

Civilians and soldiers were warned about giving information to strangers. Two slogans were readily shown on posters.

"Careless talk costs lives".
"Be like dad keep mum".

This second slogan in this day and age would be considered sexist but pre-war most married women stayed at home to look after the family. The war changed that. Women teachers replaced men who had been called up. Women started to do men's work in the factories. In the factories there would be loudspeakers. Each day they would be switched on when the radio played 'Music While You Work'. All the popular songs and tunes would be heard and the music was a stimulus to the overworked men and women.

In the evenings J.B. Priestley regularly gave talks which helped to boost morale. In the mornings the radio doctor would give advice about how to keep healthy and how to use your ration of food. As a result more people were healthier than every before and probably ever since. The practice started of news readers being readily identified by name so that propaganda broadcasting by Germans would not be mistaken for news. For Charlie and many others it was strange to hear a new announcer called Wilfred

Pickles who spoke with a broad Yorkshire accent as distinct from the southern accents of the other announcers.

Early in October, Charlie was told that he was to join a cadre of officers and non commissioned officers to go to Yeovil to train a new intake of conscripts to form a new searchlight battery. Once again he found himself entering a new situation.

Chapter 10

The cadre that went to Yeovil consisted of officers, non commissioned officers and some gunners. Charlie was the youngest person in the party and was the only person who had not been in the TA in London. They had a week to prepare themselves for the intake of about three hundred conscripts. The permanent staff at Yeovil had been through the process before and knew how to proceed with the registration and training of conscripts. Charlie made friends with a young officer on the permanent staff who had been a pupil at Stowe School. He was mortified when he saw one of his old teachers coming in as one of the conscripts. The person he had called Sir, was now to salute him and call him Sir. Fortunately the ex-teacher did not stay long with them. He was sent to OCTU.

The new entrants were given intelligence tests and tests on skills they had. One of the conscripts from Glasgow was obviously very backward and Charlie being the only Scottish officer was asked to question him. Charlie asked him some very simple questions about Glasgow and some of the footballers. He really didn't know very much and it was decided he would be better back in Civvy Street. Another who returned to civilian life was a Gypsy whose job was to go round buying and selling gold-trinkets. He couldn't read the daily orders. The other soldiers in his group said that he had 'worked his ticket' but really a person who can't read is likely to be a liability.

The conscripts were all aged about thirty one. Most of them were married with children. They were well behaved and prepared to do their best.

While they were at Yeovil, Charlie met a friend who was in his squad at Stobs Camp. This lad worked in the quartermaster's store

36

and Charlie used to pop in to see him and talk about the time they had in the militia.

The men who had been called up came from all walks of life and all parts of Britain. One man came from the Outer Hebrides and another, Gunner McPhee was a tinker who was reputed to live in a cave near Thurso. He played the bagpipes and later when they were deployed on sites in Yorkshire he found himself in trouble from the others. It was believed by them that every time he played the pipes they would have air raid alerts that night. These alerts were called 'Rousers.

After a few months of training the battery was ready for action. They were sent to Hatfield Camp, near Doncaster to take over the sites from another unit. Charlie's troop consisted of six searchlight detachments. He had a cluster of three lights at Boston Park outside Lindholme Aerodrome and another three lights at a mining village called Moorends near Thorne. Compared with London, life was quite peaceful. They would be alerted when German bombers passed on their way to Sheffield or Leeds. Sometimes they were required to use their lights to form homing beacons for bombers returning from bombing Germany.

The OC Major Carey went to regimental HQ to become second in command of the regiment. Captain P.Brown took over command. Percy had been brought up in Manchester and in time moved up through the ranks of the Greyhound Racing Association to become racing manager at the White City track. The chairman of the GRA was a Brigadier Critchley from the First World War, who had insisted that his staff joined the TA. Charlie's new unit was 518 Searchlight Battery and most of the sergeants had been kennel lads at the GRA. They had exercised the greyhounds and paraded them round the track at race meetings. The GRA was run like a military unit and so the peace time kennel lads were well prepared for army life.

Percy was a very popular officer. He had a batman called Jackie Brand who was a bit of a comedian. The two of them would write sketches for camp concerts and produced a pantomime for Christmas, which was shown in the NAAFI hall. The stage was only about two feet high and Percy wanted to give the impression that the small orchestra was in an orchestra pit so he had the legs sawn off some chairs and put a canvas screen in front to make it look right. How comfortable the orchestra was, was another matter.

During the war there was a radio programme called Ack Ack Beer Beer. Ack Ack was the radio code for Anti Aircraft and Beer Beer was Barrage Balloons. Since many of those units were in lonely sites the B.B.C. asked people to come and perform. Percy and his batman wrote a script for a programme which they performed on the radio.

Charlie's troop sergeant, Sgt. McGeachin was a Glaswegian who had been a kennel lad at White City, He was quite intelligent and he and Charlie's batman Len Eaves, looked after young Charlie with affection.

Another character was Lt. 'Pop' Deen. He was an old Etonian, whose family had estates in the Dutch East Indies. At the start of the war he was a gunner. He was on a site with eleven others. They had no cook so it was decided that each of them would take a turn at doing the day's cooking. When it was Pop's turn he took them all to the Savoy. On the occasion of the Eton - Harrow cricket match, Pop came in his top hat and tails to march up to the pay table to salute and receive his ten shillings pay.

While Charlie was at Boston Park a group of soldiers thought it might be a good idea if a battery magazine was produced. This would help to keep the various detachments on their different sites in touch with each other. Charlie's troop clerk, John S. Coventry became editor and the magazine was called 'On Target'. John was a local government officer who would not take promotion. His army pay was made up to his local authority pay by the authority and he felt that the promotion should go to someone else who needed it more.

The magazine was produced monthly and proved to be a great success. It was partly funded by adverts from two local cinemas and a pub.

Len Eaves was a regular contributor who wrote under the synonym 'T.N.F.N.' which he said meant 'Take No Further Notice'. The following is one of his pieces.

ALIAS CHARLIE

One day last week I rode to York
Where Turpin rode, and I'm sorry
For he rode there on Bonny Black Bess
While I rode on the back of a lorry.

For to ride to York on a horse's back
In a nice easy saddle is good
But to ride in a lorry is rather rough
When there's nothing to sit on but wood.

My back is still sore, my head it still aches
Since then not a word have I spoken
My teeth are all loose, I've a pain in my neck
And my tonsils are battered and broken.

One thing it has taught me - I must get a stripe
For with me went a Lance-Bombardier
Who sat in a nice cushy seat in the front
While I bumped about in the rear".

In time many people left the battery to go to other units. Pop
Deen went to Brigade HQ. Len Eaves left to become a manager in
a large NAAFI store. New young officers arrived and Charlie was
moved to battery HQ in Hatfield where the most important thing
in Charlie's life was about to happen.

Chapter 11

In May 1941 Charlie moved to battery HQ. He and Percy Brown were the only two officers left in the battery from the original cadre. Here he acted as Percy's assistant. Many new young officers had come from O.C.T.U. and they were now in charge of the three troops.

Battery HQ was the centre for communications with the troop headquarters and the sites. It was where the B.S.M. and B.Q.M.S. ruled. They saw to discipline and equipment. There was a large garage where repairs were carried out to vehicles and equipment.

Attached to the battery HQ was a platoon of ATS. These young ladies were volunteers who ran the cookhouse, served as secretaries and telephonists and drove some of the cars.

On the site was a large NAAFI where you could buy refreshments and alcohol. The NAAFI was housed in a large hall where visiting concert parties came to perform and where dances were held. Usually there were a number of other officers attached to the battery HQ. There was the medical officer, usually a padre sometimes a Catholic or sometimes Church of England or Church of Scotland.

On the 10th July, 1941 Charlie persuaded the R.C. padre to go with him, after dinner in the Officers' Mess, to a dance being held in the NAAFI. The padre wouldn't dance but liked his liquor. About 9 p.m. a young ATS girl called Hilda came into the NAAFI. It was her 19th birthday and she had been home to her parents' house in Doncaster. Finding nobody in the ATS quarters she had come over to the dance.

When she came in Charlie liked the look of her and asked her to dance. She wasn't a good dancer and they kept getting tangled up which caused them to start giggling. When the dance was over

ALIAS CHARLIE

Charlie escorted her back to the ATS quarters and much to her surprise gave her a goodnight kiss.

Hilda was one of the typists and Charlie arranged for her to work as his secretary. Soon they started to go out together and found a very strong mutual attraction.

Hilda had been a Yorkshire Schools swimming champion. Each year Doncaster schools had a swimming gala. Winners of the trophies were given season tickets to the swimming baths. Hilda and her sister May won a season ticket every year. After school they spent all their spare time there. They formed a group with some of the lads who had season tickets. Hilda's elder brother Frank had been called up into the peace time Militia. When the war started the lads from the swimming club went into the army, Hilda decided she would join the army too, so in April 1941 she went to 10 AA Division HQ at York to do her basic training.

In June 1941 she was posted to Hatfield Camp. Charlie hadn't really noticed her until the dance. They started courting, going to the cinema, going for walks in the country and swimming in the open air pool at Hatfield. They used every opportunity to be together. Charlie persuaded Hilda to go with him to York for a 24 hour leave. After that the relationship began to be physical. Hilda lost her innocence.

On Thursday 2nd October, 1941 Charlie was on a radio location course at Gainsborough in Lincolnshire. When the lectures had finished at 4 p.m. he dashed back to the Officers' Mess to listen to the Ack Ack Beer Beer programme which was being broadcast on the radio. The performers were from 518 S.L. Battery, organised by Percy Brown and Jackie Brand. Percy sang his party piece. "I'll be out in the lifeboat all night when the filleted lady goes by". Jackie performed some comedy rather nervously but the highlight for Charlie was a sketch called "Over the garden wall". Before the war this was done by Norman Evans and partner on the wireless. This time however it was being done by Hilda and her friend Jean Butler. They were two middle aged ladies gossiping over the garden wall. In more recent years this sketch has been performed on TV by Les Dawson and Roy Barraclough acting as the two old ladies.

Hilda and Jean received a cheque for three guineas from the BBC and a letter of congratulation from the divisional commander.

It became apparent that Hilda and Charlie were very attached to each other. The ATS officer did not like the idea of one of her girl privates going out with an officer who was senior to her. She arranged for her to be transferred and Hilda found herself posted to 2 AA Corps. HQ School of Technical Instruction based at Whatton, near Nottingham. This unit was the base to which many entertainers returned when they came back from entertaining troops at home and abroad. Many, in time, were to become quite famous but at that time Hilda thought they were a very ordinary lot.

The separation made the relationship even more passionate. They would try to arrange to be on 24 hour leave at the same

Private Dunhill

Bob and Hilda

time. They would spend the night in some suitable hotel in Nottingham or other places nearby.

Charlie moved out to a village, North Cave, which was near Hull to take charge of a troop which was replacing a battery which had been situated there. The North Cave troop covered a large area. It had a radar station giving early warning to the searchlight sites. Two other officers were attached to this HQ both were older and married but Charlie was in command. The troop came to be known as the 'Cavemen'.

Church parades were a good method of bringing men from the different sites to meet each other again. At North Cave the previous unit had held their parades at the C of E Church. Charlie decided to hold one at the Methodist Church. The Methodists saw this as one in the eye for the C of E. After the service the soldiers were taken into the church hall where a feast of food had been prepared. Needless to say the Methodist Church became the preferred place for church parades.

Chapter 12

At North Cave the local butcher and his wife befriended Charlie and Hilda. Each week Charlie would go to their house and enjoy the luxury of a good soak in a hot bath. Whenever Hilda came they would put her up for the night and provide breakfast free of charge.

In August 1942 Hilda went to the Northern Command School of Physical Training in Newcastle to become a PT teacher.

On the 5th September they arranged to meet in York and get engaged. Hilda chose a solitaire diamond which was quite expensive. That evening they went to the theatre to see the

*Whistefield Loch Long
1942*

ALIAS CHARLIE

JB Priestley comedy 'The Roundabout'. When they returned to their hotel they knew they were finally committed to each other.

When Charlie was at Hatfield he had taken over duties as sports officer in addition to his other duties. When the regiment decided to have a Sports Meeting at Worksop, Charlie had to arrange to get competitors for the various events. One event was a 16 mile walk. Each battery was supposed to supply a team consisting of an officer and eight other ranks. At the meeting Charlie's team was the only complete team. No other battery supplied an officer. The route had been planned by the RSM and in the programme four hours had been allocated for the walk. The fact that they arrived back after three hours when other events were on surprised the organisers.

Having won the regimental walk they were chosen to represent the regiment in the brigade competition. Then they represented the brigade at the divisional meeting in York. This time they were no longer competing against anti-aircraft units but against commandos and infantrymen. They didn't win but they still did the walk in well under three hours.

In May 1942 the tenth and last issue of 'On Target' was produced. There was a shortage of paper nationally and they weren't able to get any more.

In November 1942 Charlie was sent on an officers' PT course at Aldershot. The course lasted a month and the officers were split into two squads, Charlie's squad was under the control of Tommy Lawton the England centre forward. The course was fairly demanding. One event was walking along a high rope stretching between trees. You held on to a rope about six feet above the rope you walked on. One officer who was quite athletic in other events was terrified of heights and wouldn't attempt to do it. Being tall was a disadvantage. One exercise involved raising logs above your head and moving them from shoulder to shoulder. A team of six officers lifted the log. Charlie and one other six footer bore the brunt of the weight while the smaller officers had it easy. On the combat course there was a competition against the other squad. This involved getting through and over various obstacles. One was a high wall. The tallest person, Charlie, had to stand at the wall whilst the other climbed over him and up to the wall top. When all the others had got over Charlie had to run and jump and catch on to the hands of two who were hanging over the wall to pull him up. As the result depended on the time of the first and the last Charlie had to do his best to beat the last man in the other squad.

On many afternoons they had to take to the boxing ring. They would box against each other for three, one minute rounds. They would take their turn at refereeing and judging each bout. Charlie qualified to become a referee and judge of boxing.

One afternoon they went on a cross country run. This was never Charlie's best event. As he and another plodded along at the tail, the medical officer joined them. He was Jack Lovelock the New Zealander who had won the mile at the last Olympic Games. His legs were a little thicker than Charlie's arms. He chatted to them for a while then decided to accelerate away so easily.

They did survival exercises including swimming. One afternoon a psychiatrist came to explain how important it was for an officer to lead his men. In difficult situations it was the willpower of the officer which would get the men doing what was required. To demonstrate willpower he invited a volunteer to come out. He intended to make him do something he didn't want to do. Unfortunately for him the volunteer matched him in will power, Charlie was glad he hadn't volunteered.

When the course finished Charlie met Hilda in London. They spent the night at the Strand Palace Hotel. Before that they went to see "The Dancing Years", starring Ivor Novello at the Adelphi Theatre. Ivor Novello didn't appear. He was in prison. Petrol was rationed and you had to have coupons. Ivor was given some petrol coupons by a lady admirer. It was illegal to use someone else's coupons thus it was that his part was played by an understudy.

On the train back to Doncaster, Charlie went to the first class toilet. Sitting on the coach was Clement Attlee, the deputy prime minister, who was working on some papers. He didn't appear to have any security guards with him.

At Christmas 1942 they spent Christmas Day with Hilda's family in Doncaster then went to Clydebank. Charlie's parents' home had been destroyed during the bombing. On the second night his mother was so tired she wanted to sleep in her own bed. Fortunately she was persuaded to go into the brick shelter in the street else she would have lost her life. They were now living in a rented detached bungalow.

Chapter 13

Stationed at Louth with Hilda was a Danish girl who had married the major from Sunderland who had been in charge of the battery in Ripon when Charlie was at Thirsk. She had this beautiful wedding dress made in Denmark but which had arrived too late for her own wedding. She asked Hilda if she would like to wear it.

For the wedding Hilda was given a month's leave and Charlie had a week's leave. They were married on a beautiful March morning in the Parish Church at Doncaster. Hilda's eldest sister Eve was matron of honour. Major Percy Brown was best man and Pop Deen also came to the wedding. The reception was held at the Danum Hotel, Danum being the old name for Doncaster.

The first night of the honeymoon was spent at Young's Hotel in St. Petersgate in York. The bill with 5% gratuities amounted to £1 8s. 6d.

In earlier years Young's Hotel had been the home of St. Peter's School whose most famous pupil was Guy Fawkes. To this day Guy Fawkes Day is never celebrated at St. Peter's School.

The following day they travelled to Clydebank where Charlie's relations gathered to give them a second wedding reception. The following day they went to the Colquhoun Arms in Luss on Loch Lomond to spend the rest of the honeymoon. The weather continued to be warm and sunny. Everywhere daffodils were in flower. The weather could not have been better.

When they got back Hilda found accommodation with a lady in Grimsby very near to Charlie's HQ. Each night Charlie would slip out of his HQ to go to sleep with Hilda and it was there that their first child was conceived.

Hilda returned to her unit which was now at Digby and shortly afterwards Charlie was posted to a S.L. regiment near Hull. His new troop HQ was at Sunk Island. He had never met such a

ALIAS CHARLIE

Arundel, West Sussex
1963

lethargic group of soldiers. When they got a 24 hour leave they couldn't be bothered going into Hull. Mind you Hull was in a bit of a mess. German bomber crews were often sent to bomb Hull on their first mission. It was so easy to fly along the Humber and find the way back to Germany.

Charlie had been sent to this regiment because they were being reorganized to become a mobile anti-aircraft unit. Some of their older officers and soldiers were to be posted out and fit young men like Charlie were brought in.

Shortly afterwards the regiment was replaced and moved to a camp nearby ready for the reorganisation. Charlie did not join the main group but was sent with a captain and the men who were to be posted out, to a derelict camp site. This captain was being transferred, Charlie thought he was a little effeminate. He would only drink Earl Grey tea.

Two weeks later they were all dispatched to their new units and

Charlie returned to join the main regiment. Whilst Charlie had been away new troops were formed. Searchlight troops had a lieutenant in charge but LAA troops had a captain. Much to Charlie's disgust he found that the people promoted to captain were all junior to him. They had been with the regiment for a longer time and Charlie, the newcomer, was passed over.

The regiment were Sherwood Foresters and wore a green diamond on the back of the battledress. The tradition was that if you turned your back and started to run from the enemy the green diamond would give them a good target.

At the end of April a new colonel was appointed to take over command of the regiment. He was John Widgery who had been the assistant adjutant in the LEE in London. In civilian life he had been a solicitor. After the war he trained to become a barrister and moved on to eventually become Lord Chief Justice.

At the beginning of May the new regiment, 149 LAA Regiment Royal Artillery went to Holywood Barracks near Belfast, the same barracks where Lord Chief Justice Widgery held the 'Bloody Sunday' investigation many years later. The regiment was being trained to use Bofors guns which fired 40 mm. shells.

Life in Belfast was lovely. There seemed to be no rationing. Food was plentiful. On a Saturday aftenoon Charlie and his friends would take the short train journey into Belfast. They would have a 'high tea' in some restaurant, then on to the Grand Opera House to see whatever show was on. After the show they would go for dinner at one of the best hotels.

On Sundays they would go by train to Bangor for a walk along the sea front and a good meal somewhere. During the week they worked hard getting to know the Bofors gun and other equipment.

There came a time when they went out on a scheme. The order of travelling was made out. Charlie's battery would lead. Charlie's troop would be the first troop and Charlie's section would be the first section, which meant that Charlie had to lead the whole regiment consisting of fifty four lorries towing Bofors guns and other lorries and vehicles used by the regiment.

Charlie in his utility van did the map reading whilst his driver drove the van. All road signs had been removed throughout

Northern Ireland as had been done in Great Britain. In those days he was unaware that he had an astigmatism which meant that symbols on the map were not always clearly seen. He proceeded along this road knowing that he had to take a right turn at the next main road. He turned right at what seemed to be a main road. All the other vehicles followed him. The road started to peter out after a while. They were now travelling on bare rock over a mountain. John Widgery was on a motorbike and he drove on in front to see what lay ahead. Charlie kept going. The thought that all these vehicles and guns might need to be manhandled around to go back was frightening. Charlie thought if the colonel wants me to stop he'll say so. They continued the journey over the mountain and as they got further down the road started to improve.

No mention was made of the route Charlie had taken. Secretly the colonel was pleased to see how his regiment coped with the situation.

Early in June 1943 the regiment moved to a little fishing village, Ardglass where there was a firing camp. An aeroplane would fly slowly over the sea towing a long sleeve called a drogue. The guns each had a chance of firing shells at the drogue. Amongst the shells were tracer shells which lit up showing the path being taken. An optical illusion takes place as the shells go towards the target. The plane would be flying from right to left. At first the shells appear to be going straight but as they approached the sleeve they seemed to go on a curve to the right. What was happening was that the shells kept going straight but as one looked at the target the shells were moving right relative to the drogue. Barely was the sleeve hit and rarely was sufficient aim off allowed for the speed of the target. It made Charlie wonder if we can't hit a slow moving drogue what chance have we of hitting a fast moving fighter aircraft.

After Ardglass they went back to Holywood Barracks where they had a ceremonial dinner before returning to England.

Chapter 14

When Hilda realised she was pregnant she went to see the Army doctor who confirmed that she was. At that time Charlie was in Northern Ireland. Hilda was released from the army on 12th June, 1943 just before her 21st birthday. Hilda stayed with her parents for the first week then went to Clydebank to live with Charlie's parents.

Charlie's parents were pleased to have her. In one way they saw her as a replacement for Charlie's sister Nessie. Charlie's two sisters left school at fourteen and went to work in chemists' shops. When the war broke out many pharmacists went into the forces. Nessie, the elder sister, took a job with a big Glasgow chemist. She was in charge of the stores, ordering supplies and ensuring that they had sufficient stocks of medicines. She worked long hours and travelled to and from work in the dark of winter. Unfortunately, she caught a tuberculosis germ resulting in Galloping Consumption for which there was no known cure. She died in August 1940.

The loss of Nessie and the fact that Charlie was an officer in the Army, with the memories of how young officers died in the First World War, was a most harrowing time for Marion and Tom. Before the war, Marion was a very attractive young looking mother. The war rapidly aged her. Her hazel brown hair went grey and there was a secret grief and fear.

After the destructive bombing in which many Clydebank people lost their lives, they were living in a nice bungalow. Anne the younger sister was being courted by a doctor. His surgery was a few doors away from the chemist's where Anne worked. He found it very convenient to pop in daily to be served by this young attractive assistant. John and Anne started to go out together and he was the doctor who delivered Hilda's child, Susan.

ALIAS CHARLIE

One day when Charlie was home on leave, an RAF sergeant hailed him from across the road. Charlie went over to speak to him. He didn't recognise the sergeant. His face was very badly scarred and he had lost his Clydebank accent. He was a member of a bomber crew whose plane had been severely damaged. He seemed to know Charlie well but Charlie couldn't make out who he was. After they had parted Charlie realised he had been talking to 'Cuddy' Mair with whom he had played rugby at school and after they had left school. Sometime later Charlie was saddened to hear that Flight Lieutenant Mair had been killed on a bombing mission

On another occasion he and Hilda were in Glasgow when they met a pal who was now an Army padre. He said how sad he was to hear about John Kinloch. He said, John had been an army officer killed in North Africa. Charlied refused to believe him. It must be John's cousin. If John had been killed his mother would have told him. When he got home he questioned his mother who confirmed the fact. She didn't want Charlie to be upset by hearing about the loss of his best friend.

As the war progressed Charlie learned of the death of more of his friends.

Sgt Gordon McRobert killed flying a Blenheim off the coast of Holland.
Sgt Jim Forrest killed in action with the RAF.
Sgt Observer Douglas Allen killed in action in the Middle East.
Petty Officer Leslie Murgatroyd killed at sea.
Sgt Hugh Third, RAF killed in action over enemy territory.
Sgt Pilot Jack Little RAF shot down and killed over France.
Sgt Observer Alistair Skinner killed in action.

They were a great bunch of lads.

Alistair Skinner always arrived at school at the very last minute. He was never late. It was funny to see pupils running past Alistair to make sure they weren't late and put in detention.

Throughout the country there were hundreds of thousands of lads like them who gave their all for their country and we should never forget that.

Susan was born on 23rd December, 1943. At that time Charlie was stationed at Eastbourne in what had been a big hotel on the seafront. About two weeks later he got leave to go up to see his young daughter and Hilda. What a good Christmas present to have, a beautiful young baby.

When Charlie got back to Eastbourne the unit moved to Swanage, in Dorset. Charlie thought Swanage was one of the most beautiful places he'd been to. In those days there was little commercialism there. The whole of the South Coast was protected by barbed wire fencing and many of the beaches were mined in case the enemy attempted to land.

Growing under the barbed wire were mushrooms called bluestalks which were very tasty with a bit of fried bacon.

While at Swanage, Charlie was sent on a waterproofing course at Rhyl in Wales. He was taught how to waterproof vehicles so that when they come off a landing craft they could be driven through water on to the beach.

Shortly afterwards Charlie's troop left the Sherwood Foresters to join an LAA regiment (The Buffs) in Great Yarmouth. There the troop was converted from Bofors Guns to 20 mm Oerliken guns mounted on the backs of trucks. The idea was that in mobile warfare an army column needed protection from enemy aircraft and these guns would be interspersed in the column.

There now began a period of waiting and manoeuvres. Charlie's troop was supposed to be the enemy. Charlie was killed twice before being captured in one of the manoeuvres.

The South Coast and East Coast of England were packed solid with British, American, Canadian and Polish troops together with the Free French forces under General De Gaulle, all waiting for the anticipated landing in Europe.

Hilda by now had moved back to Doncaster where she shared a rented house with another army officer's wife and young son. Civilians were not allowed to come into the invasion area from outside. Charlie managed to get a 24 hour leave and met Hilda in Norwich which was just outside the exclusion area. Susan was left with Hilda's sister, May, for that short break.

Shortly afterwards it was announced that on June 6th, 1944 the

Allied invasion of Normandy had started. Now it was a matter of waiting for the off.

Chapter 15

Charlie's troop was part of 89 LAA Regt. RA, which was attached to 56 Infantry Brigade of the 49th (Polar Bear) Division. The division got this name because of their fight in Norway against the invasion by the Germans. The divisional badge was a polar bear standing on a block of ice. 49 Division was involved in some very heavy fighting early in the battle in Normandy. The Germans called them The Polar Bear Butchers a nickname which the division accepted as a matter of pride.

The mobile troop of 20 mm guns was not immediately needed so they waited anxiously round Yarmouth for about three weeks before they started their journey to Tilbury Docks, in London, where they embarked on a Liberty ship. They sailed down the Thames then along a route which was surrounded by hundreds of naval ships for three days before they arrived near Arromanches in Normandy. They disembarked on to a newly constructed pier so there was no need for all the vehicle waterproofing.

They were met by a major, who was part of the advance party and led to an area near Dovres where the rest of the battery were assembled. They were far enough away from the battlefront not to be in any particular danger. On the evening of their arrival a German bomber flew over to be met by a barrage from anti-aircraft guns and from naval ships. In fact, the ships were inclined to fire at any plane whether it be friend or foe. Allied aircraft were easily identified by the broad white stripes on their wings.

A few days later Charlie's guns were deployed almost on the front line. Charlie led his three anti-aircraft guns to their positions under heavy mortar fire. When they were in position he had to jump into a shell hole where two infantry soldiers were sheltering from the bombardment. When things had quietened he crept forward to check on his gunners. He had difficulty finding them.

ALIAS CHARLIE

They were buried deep in the ground. When they were on exercises in England they took ages to dig themselves in. Under the heavy fire they managed to do in minutes what would have taken hours in England.

On his crawling journey he met a young artillery officer who was in a forward observation post. He was spotting where the British shells were landing. Charlie felt sorry for him. He was in such a dangerous position and to add to his troubles he said he was a vegetarian and the only foods he was getting were tins of corned beef and beef stew. All the vegetables were dehydrated and the packet of cabbage looked like cornflakes.

Charlie made his way back to his HQ where Sam, his batman driver, had been left to dig a slit trench big enough for the two of them. He had been told to dig it under the cover of a railway embankment which provided shelter from the enemy guns. When Charlie got back he found that Sam had dug the trench in the middle of the field. He hadn't been able to get a place near the railway. It was fortunate that he did. Unbeknown to everyone there was a German gun on the flank and it started shelling along the line where everyone was taking cover.

After 24 hours somebody in authority realised it was pointless having 20mm Oerliken guns so far forward. They were of no use there and besides the Allied Air Force was now dominating the skies. The order came for Charlie's troop to return to regimental HQ. It was decided that the troop should return to England to train to be infantry. However, Charlie was to go to Divisional HQ to become a liaison officer. Charlie's troop sergeant had been with him a long time and he was given the option of returning to England to train to become an infantry officer or staying as a sergeant with the Bofors guns. He and Charlie discussed the matter very fully and they both thought that staying with the Bofors guns would be safer than changing to an infantry officer. Sgt. Holland decided to stick with the guns. Two months later Charlie learned that Sgt. Holland had been killed.

Charlie presented himself at Divisional HQ to become the new liaison officer. An LO was basically an errand boy. In the morning he would go with his map which had been marked by the duty officer to the HQ of other divisions or brigades. He clearly remembers going to the HQ of the Airborne Division for their 10 a.m. briefing. What he learned he would pass on to the duty officer to amend the main map. During the day he would take a stint of being duty officer keeping the map up to date and informing his superiors of information coming from other units either by radio or by dispatch riders.

In the evening he would be asked to deliver the orders for the following day to some regiment or brigade HQ. One evening at about 11 p.m. he was sent to the HQ of the Reconnaisance Regiment with the orders for the following day. He was given the map reference where they would be. This HQ consisted of a few heavily camouflaged armoured cars. Charlie went to find them in the dark. Map reading was not Charlie's strong point. He went along this lane and across the field he saw shadows of what he took to be the vehicles of the Recce Regiment. He went across the field in the dark and as he got nearer he realised he was looking at some haystacks. As he made his way back to his Jeep he remembered that he had climbed over some barbed wire to get into the field. Barbed wire was often a sign that an area had been mined. Charlie thought what do I do now? He decided that all he could do was take very long steps and hope for the best.

When he got to his Jeep his radio was buzzing, "Where the hell are you"? The Recce Regt. were waiting for their orders.

Charlie was working very long hours and had to grab what little sleep he could get. One night he was left in charge of the division. The general was asleep, the G.1, the G.2 and all the staff captains were abed. Charlie was in this caravan in the heat and in dim light, hearing all sorts of messaages over the radio. He was very tired. At 2 a.m. the code had to be changed. This was done daily so that the enemy wouldn't understand the coded messages being sent out. Charlie started making the changes whilst nodding off to sleep. Shortly afterwards he was relieved by a staff captain who took over the duties. He played hell with Charlie the following day. When he came on duty he had checked the new code and found some mistakes.

One of the good things about being an LO was that you were

kept well informed about what was happening all along the front line. One day the American Air Force bombed US troops by mistake. This could never happen with the British Air Force thought Charlie or could it?

The German army was in retreat and an attempt was to be made to trap them in the Falaise Gap. 49 Division was to lead the drive to get to Falaise. The Polish Armoured Brigade were to head the attack and they were positioned in some quarries along the way. A thousand British bombers were to be used to bomb the German positions. The first planes came over and dropped coloured smoke signals to identify the targets. Unfortunately, some landed where the Poles were waiting . For the next hour Lancaster and Halifax bombers came flying over and dropped their bombs on the areas marked by the smoke. When it was realised they were bombing our own troops there was no way of stopping them. An Auster spotting plane was sent up to try to get them to move away but they kept on bombing relentlessly. Apparently there was no way of communicating with them except by sending messages to England and by the time the messages got through the bombing was over.

Some war reporters had gone to one quarry to see the start of the operation. They came back to Divisional HQ cursing the Air Force. The reporter from the Daily Mirror was going to tell his paper all about the cock up. Needless to say not a word appeared in any newspaper.

Chapter 16

Some fifty five years later Charlie still has memories of his time in Normandy. A few days after he had landed he was sent back to the beachhead to await the arrival of the remainder of the regiment. He had a very long wait by which time he was becoming quite hungry. After enquiries he was directed to an army hut where they were doling out a tin of bully beef, an army biscuit and a mug of tea. The army biscuit was about three inches square, half an inch thick and as hard as rock. This with the corned beef was one of the most enjoyable meals Charlie ever had.

Bayeux had been captured but Caen still had to be taken. The only drink available seemed to be a rough clear spirit, Calvados, which was a distillation of cider. Everywhere there were orchards but all the apples were bitter cider apples. Each farm had its own cider press and barrels of the stuff. Charlie had the impression that the farmers were rarely sober.

One evening he saw a farmer walking beside his wife. She was carrying a yoke on her shoulders. Each side of the yoke was attached to a bucket of milk swarming with flies. The farmer strolled along with his hands in his pockets while his wife struggled to carry the milk which she'd got by milking the cows in the field.

Charlie clearly remembers cattle standing shivering in the fields while shells were being exchanged. One farmer whose farm was in the German side of the front managed to cross over to the British sector. He was at great pains to point out the various farms where the Germans were. His farm he pointed out had no Germans. There was no need to shell there.

Near the beachhead were little lads aged about 8 to 12 years old, begging from soldiers. The two most common requests were, "Cigarettes pour papa", and "Jig a Jig with sister."

ALIAS CHARLIE

In the area near Caen every house seemed to have been destroyed either by shelling or bombing. The area was a dust bowl. There were no birds. At night Charlie and his soldiers slept in slit trenches. Mosquitos were everywhere and they left swollen bits of flesh where they had bitten. In an attempt to keep the mosquitos out of the slit trenches, lace curtains from the empty houses were used to cover the trenches but still a mosquito would find its way in.

Charlie remembers one journey where many vehicles were on the move. At a crossroad there was a military policeman, red cap, directing the traffic. The crossroad was easily seen by the Germans and they kept dropping shells there. He often wondered if that red cap survived.

As they kept going forward their progress would be halted by a blown up bridge over some small river. Charlie never realised there could be so many canals and rivers to be crossed. Each night the Royal Engineers would construct a bridge usually under heavy gunfire. The next day they would travel to the next river and the process of bridge building would take place.

Charlie's days as a liaison officer were soon to end. One afternoon he was told to take a map of the divisional positions to the tactical HQ of the Corps Commander. Senior officers usually had tactical Headquarters which were much nearer the front than the main HQ. Charlie had his map marked in the operations room and set off to get to Corps tactical HQ. He found himself on a lane behind a group of Churchill tanks which were moving very slowly. There was no way of overtaking them so Charlie arrived later than intended. He went to the ops. room and was taken directly to the Corps Commander. General Horrocks then began to question him in detail. Charlie didn't know all the answers to his specific questions.

The Corps Commander must have sent a rocket to Div. HQ for sending such an incompetent LO Charlie was interviewed by G.1 who told him to stop wearing his silly peaked cap. A few days later Charlie was transferred to 56 Brigade HQ to become a Counter Mortar Officer.

This was a new small unit comprising a major, Charlie, a small

HQ staff and three armoured car crews. Basically the idea was very simple. The three armoured vehicles would be placed up near the front line. There they would listen to enemy mortars being fired and using a small prismatic compass they would take a bearing on the mortars. This would be radioed back to Charlie. He had a map covered with transparent celluloid on which was marked the location of the three sites. As a mortar fired each site would send in a bearing. If these three bearings crossed at a point, a message would be sent to the field guns who would proceed to shell that point. Although it was done in a very simple way it turned out to be very effective and many enemy mortars were destroyed.

One day Charlie was leading one of the vehicles to its new position. When the crew got there they complained that somebody had been firing a machine gun and the bullets kept going in front of them. Apparently the Germans were shooting at Charlie in his Jeep but they were not allowing for the speed of his vehicle so the bullets were missing him. He was unaware that he had been seen and shot at by the Germans.

49 Division was commanded by Major General 'Bubbles' Barker. He was called 'Bubbles' after the Gainsborough picture which appeared on the wrapper of Pears soap. As a child he had been the 'Bubbles' on the wrapper. In action he was no 'Bubbles'. He was fearless and was always to be found up near the front.

The division moved up through Normandy until they reached the River Seine on 29th August. The Seine has huge bends or links as it wends its way to the sea. In one of these bends was the Foret de Bretonne. As the brigade moved up through the forest to the river they found the area littered with abandoned guns and vehicles. There were dead German soldiers, dead horses, everything had been abandoned in an attempt to cross the river. As there was no bridge there, the only way of escape was to make rafts and float across.

Attached to 56 Brigade was an American Civil Affairs Officer called Alan Lund who in peace time was a lawyer in Hollywood. Alan and Charlie were good friends. When the forest was cleared of German troops the brigade started to make its way to Rouen.

ALIAS CHARLIE

All the bridges over the Seine had been blown up by the enemy but there was a railway bridge which the Royal Engineers had repaired by putting a Bailey bridge across the damaged part.

Alan and Charlie decided to see if they could get some fresh eggs from one of the farms. Having got the eggs they joined the queue of vehicles making for Rouen. Eventually they got to the railway marshalling yard to take their turn to cross the river. When they had reached the start of the bridge they saw the repaired part collapse under the weight of vehicles.

Alan and Charlie found themselves separated from the main part of the brigade HQ and worst thing of all the ration wagons were on the other side of the river. It took almost a day for the vehicles behind them to turn round and make their way to another repaired bridge. During that day the two of them existed on a diet of boiled eggs.

After crossing the River Seine the division made its way towards the next objective, the capture of Le Havre.

Chapter 17

The port of Le Havre was heavily defended. It was an important German naval base and the capture of the port would enable the allies to receive some of the supplies that were urgently needed to support the drive towards Belgium and Holland.

Charlie's unit was given a new task, instead of trying to find mortar positions they were to locate the positions of German AA guns. This time these positions were mapped but not shelled.

On 5th September, Alan and Charlie were 'swanning' around in Charlie's Jeep when they came to a small town, Montevilliers. As they entered, the crowds came out to give them a great welcome. Apparently the German forces had left an hour before they arrived and they were the first Allied troops to enter the town. In the centre some young women were having all their hair shaved off. They were guilty of having consorted with German soldiers.

A young French lad, Olivier Dupont attached himself to them and acted as interpreter. He took them to his home to meet his parents and younger brother Michael.

Alan stayed in Montevillers to reorganise the local government. The people running the town were deemed to be 'collaborators' and were put in jail. Alan appointed the Maquis chief as military governor.

A few days later Michael was on a hill showing some officers the positions of German troops when he was shot and killed by a German sniper.

Charlie still has scraps of paper given to him by Maquis chiefs. The one from Montevilliers says, "Many thanks and best wishes. Vive les Allies."

Another reads "Mes felicitations", Cartous, chef Maquis, Cormeilles, Calvados, France.

ALIAS CHARLIE

A third was from the Maquis chief in Lisieux. He gave Charlie a leaf from a tree growing in the grounds of Lisieux cathedral. This tree had some connection with St. Therese. The leaf was in a little cellophane packet and had been carried by the Maquis chief as a good luck charm. He gave it to Charlie hoping it would bring him good luck throughout the war.

Le Havre was protected by the naval base on one side and by a range of hills on the other side. Into these hills the Germans had dug caves into which their 88 m.m. guns were installed. In front of the hills was a large minefield. It seemed that any attack would meet fierce resistance and that there would be heavy casualties. The attack was to be made by 49 Division and 51st Highland Division. Both divisions, at the time, were under the control of the Canadian Army.

At 2p.m. on the 10th September two warships, the Warspite and the Erebus started to shell the port. At the same time the field guns started shelling the town and in particular the German anti-aircraft positions. At 3 p.m. the shelling stopped and 250 bombers started to bomb the area where the German field guns were. Another 250 bombers came over at 3.15 and again at 3.30 and 3.45. In all the 1,000 Halifax and Lancasters bombed with great accuracy.

At 4 p.m. the flail tanks started to beat paths through the minefield. These tanks were specially fortified. They had big revolving drums at the front to which were attached large metal chains. These flails hit the ground with great force setting off the mines in their path. The flail tanks were followed by flame throwing tanks which sent out flames to a distance of forty feet. The flame throwers were followed by open topped tanks carrying infantry soldiers. By 4.15 p.m. the flame throwers and infantry had reached the positions of the 88 m.m guns. The Germans were still in a state of shock after all the shelling and bombing and the sight of the flames from the flame throwers was enough to cause them to surrender.

Once the outer defences had been breached the way was open for the tanks and infantry to fight their way through the town and on to the docks. Within 36 hours the battle was over. The German commander had been injured and his second in command gave the order to surrender. 49 Division took 7,000 prisoners and the 51st Highland Division about 5,000.

General Crerand, the commander of the Canadian Army sent the following message to Air Chief Marshal 'Bomber' Harris who commanded Bomber Command.

"All ranks have the highest praise for the remarkable accuracy of the bombing and the timing of every attack on the German garrison and fortified positions at Le Havre".

Charlie and his small HQ staff moved into Le Havre on the evening of the attack. They came to a square and decided to bed down there for the night. One of his lads went snooping around and reported that there was a large building with lots of empty beds, so Charlie and his men went there. True enough there were all these single rooms with nice white sheets on the beds. They had their first night's sleep on a proper bed since they had landed in Normandy.

Came the morning, they found the place swarming with nuns who had been sheltering in the cellars all night.

Charlie made some sort of apology to the Mother Superior who was only too grateful that the fighting was ending.

56 Brigade chose to make its HQ in a large fort. Down in the cellar there was a huge store of bottles of Vichy water but no alcohol. However one of the scout cars found a cave where the Germans had stored all their luxuries. A 3 ton lorry was sent to be loaded with champagne, benedictine, brandy, tins of asparagus, boxes of cigars, tins of McVities biscuits and other foods, some of which had obviously been captured from the BEF in 1940

Once the 3 tonner had returned with all its goodies, divisional HQ was informed. They sent a squad to guard the cave and during the next few days every man in the division received something from the store.

56 Brigade decided to hold a champagne party for all the officers. A lot of alcohol was consumed that night. When it was

ALIAS CHARLIE

time to move on from Le Havre, the 3 ton lorry couldn't be spared to carry the remaining booze and so each officer at brigade HQ was given a share of the booty. Charlie was given a box of cigars, two bottles of benedictine and three bottles of Armagnac brandy. Since he was a non-smoker and didn't drink much the cigars and the bottles were with him for a long time.

Chapter 18

A few days after the capture of Le Havre, Charlie witnessed a sight he would never forget. Hundreds of planes towing gliders were making their way from England to Holland. This was the start of 'Operation Market Garden', an attempt to capture the bridge at Eindhoven over the River Maas, the bridge at Nijmegen over the River Waal and the bridge over the Neder Rhine at Arnhem. The US airborne troops succeeded in capturing the bridges at Eindhoven and Nijmegen and the British 2nd Army armoured divisions secured the bridges and liberated the towns but they were meeting very strong resistance and their advance was slowed down.

The British Airborne troops captured the bridge at Arnhem but they were attacked by a superior force consisting of the 9th and 10th Panzer divisions. The Airborne division held out for twelve days hoping that the armoured divisions would come to their aid. Some of the soldiers managed to retreat to the other side of the river but the majority were killed or captured. It was a 'bridge too far'.

While this was going on 49 Division as part of the Canadian Army was helping to free the towns along the French coast. Dieppe then Abbeville, Boulogne, Calais, Dunkirk and Ostend were rapidly attacked and captured. Charlie managed to go into Dieppe and saw the huge submarine pens which were dug into the cliffs. There was no way that Allied bombers could get at the submarines when they were in their pens.

The British 2nd Army was rapidly progressing through Belgium and into Holland. Antwerp had been captured but it couldn't be used as a port until the entrance through the Scheldt Estuary had been cleared. The whole area was heavily defended. Some of the dykes were bombed to flush out German defensive positions.

ALIAS CHARLIE

Between the Canadians, fighting in the Scheldt Estuary and the British 2nd Army's progress into Holland, there was a gap. It was decided to fill this gap by using 89 LAA Regiment and a regiment of Belgium resistance soldiers, from Antwerp. The unit was called 'Bobforce' after Bob Cory the CO of 89 LAA Regiment. Charlie and his little group of radio operators and counter mortar personnel were released from 56 Brigade to form part of the HQ of Bobforce.

Bobforce held a line eight miles wide just short of the Dutch border for a period of three weeks. When American reinforcements arrived, Bobforce was disbanded. The Belgium resistance troops were to return to Antwerp and 89 LAA Regiment was to join up with the rest of 49 Division in Holland. Colonel Bob Cory decided to give a personnel message to each of the Belgium soldiers. He asked Charlie to get it translated into Flemish. Now Charlie and the Belgium commander's young son had become friends so Charlie took the message written in English to him and asked him to translate it. To Charlie's amazement he found he could only translate it into French and so they had to take the French translation to the local priest who turned it into Flemish. It seemed so strange that a young officer couldn't easily speak the language that his men spoke. It was the first time that Charlie realised that Antwerp was Flemish speaking and Brussels was French speaking.

Charlie and his men went back to join 56 Brigade as it was making its way through Holland. The brigade overcame some stiff resistance to capture the town of Roosendaal. The weather was becoming wet and cold. On one occasion Charlie and his men found a comfy place to spend the night. It was in a big Dutch barn. On the floor of the barn were cows in stalls. Above this was a balcony where straw and hay were stored. That's where they slept. It was lovely and warm and they weren't put off by the smell.

It was around this time that Charlie was required to sit on a Court Martial. Judging the case with him were a captain from another unit and a major who seemed to do nothing else but preside over these trials. The case was trivial. A soldier had stolen a pair of boots from a Dutch farmer. Charlie thought the soldier should be fined but the other two overruled him and decided that his punishment should be six months in a military prison. To Charlie going into a 'glasshouse' as they were called was like going into a Butlin's Holiday Camp compared with the conditions in Holland.

At the end of December they reached Nijmegen. The counter mortar unit had been disbanded and they were back with 89 LAA Regiment. On the first night in Nijmegen, Charlie slept at the house of a Mrs Schwartz. She told Charlie to be careful how he used the toilet. It had been damaged by some shrapnel. Next morning when Charlie sat on, the toilet bowl collapsed under his weight. It was a most embarassing experience trying to explain what had happened to Mrs Schwartz.

The following day the 31st December, 1944, Charlie and his radio operators moved into a large house owned by Mr & Mrs Bergsma. Living with them was her mother 'Dutch Granny' and their maid Annie. Mr Bergsma had worked for many years in the Dutch East Indies before setting up a little factory in Nijmegen. Mrs Bergsma was a very fine pianist and singer. 'Dutch Granny' was in her 80's, a formidable little woman as far as the Germans were concerned but very friendly to Charlie and his men.

The weather in November and December had been very wet and cold and the progress of the Canadian, British and American armies had slowed up in the mud. German resistance was fierce. The result of this was that Charlie and his group stayed much longer with the Bergsma family than they had anticipated.

The River Rhine splits into two rivers on its journey through Holland. Nijmegen stands at the southern side of the Waal and Arnhem is on the northern side of the Neder Rhine. The island between the two rivers was occupied in the South by Allied troops and in the North by German troops. The roads between the two towns were above the level of the land and were easily targeted.

At Nijmegen the railway bridge over the Waal had been blown up but the road bridge was intact. There was a fear that the Germans might succeed in destroying this bridge by floating mines down the river. A Bofors gun and a searchlight were placed to the North East of Nijmegen with instructions to fire on any large package floating down the river. The gun barrel was depressed to shoot down on to the river but sometimes a shell would ricochet off the river surface on to the other shore where British troops were dispersed.

Charlie spent many a cold winter's night in charge of the searchlight and gun. On some nights a rum issue was authorised and this helped to warm up a mug of hot tea.

Because Charlie had landed in Normandy with a troop of 20 m.m. guns which was sent back to England to train to become infantry while he stayed in France, he was a spare officer who was used to carry out duties as the occasion demanded. It was decided that 89 LAA Regiment could do with a little cafe in Nijmegen to serve cups of tea to men from the regiment who were moving around . A little cafe was re-opened and Charlie was asked to supervise its running. Some lads had been chosen to do the work but Charlie had to get the supplies. He went to Canadian Corps HQ to see if they would supply him with tea, sugar, powdered milk and packets of biscuits. Here he met unexpected hostility. "We are not giving anything to the English". "I'm not English", said Charlie. "I'm a Scot". That was different and he left with a more than adequate supply.

Life with the Bergsma family became quite comfortable. Once a week Mrs Bergsma would invite a few friends and they would have a concert. Rationing in Holland was severe and on those nights Charlie's group would draw their food from the cookhouse and share it with the group. When Holland was invaded by the Germans the Bergsma family had a large chest of tea. By the end of 1944 there was almost nothing left and the tea they were drinking was very weak indeed. This was one area where Charlie was able to help.

Mr Bergsma was a pipe smoker. As there was no tobacco in the shops, he grew his own tobacco. The loft of the house was festooned with rows of leaves hanging up to dry.

January and February were very cold and the snow lay deep. Towards the end of February things started to warm up and the snow disappeared. The Bergsmas decided that the Germans wouldn't be coming back so they asked the lads to dig up the silver and gold trinkets that they'd buried in the garden. Before the War, Dutch coins were made of silver. When the Germans came the silver coins were replaced by using a base metal.

Dutch Granny had been corresponding with Hilda in England and Hilda had sent her some warm underwear. This was repaid by having a bracelet made out of some of the pre-war guilders.

89 LAA Regiment remained in Nijmegen but Charlie and his major 'Tom' set up a tactical HQ east of Nijmegen nearer to the battlefront. Hilda's brother Frank was passing through Nijmegen when he saw the sign for 89 LAA Regiment. He enquired where Charlie was and being told, he went to the house where he was billeted. Tom, Charlie and Frank had one or two drinks together from what had been brought from Le Havre, then Frank was driven back to his field gun which was firing all night long. Charlie imagined Frank might have had a bit of a hangover the following morning.

Chapter 19

Whilst at Nijmegen Charlie was given a 36 hours leave to go to Antwerp. He and an older officer from Carlisle travelled by Jeep. On arrival in Antwerp they went to the Excelsior Hotel which was reserved for officers on leave. The first thing Charlie did was to have a good long soak in a hot bath. In Britain there was a need to restrict the unnecessary use of coal. The munitions factories were using so much that to increase coal production some men were conscripted to work in the mines rather than in the forces. These young conscripts were called 'Bevin Boys', after Ernest Bevin, the minister for labour. To be able to have a good long soak in a bath full of hot water was sheer luxury. In Britain you were expected to bathe in 5" depth of bath water.

After his bath he went to the restaurant to have some tea. Here he had his first ice cream since the start of the war. In Britain no ice cream was being sold. The reason was never clear to Charlie but a factor might have been that nearly all the ice cream shops were run by Italians who had been removed to detention in the Isle of Man. More likely was the sugar rationing.

He had tea whilst listening to a small orchestra in the dining room. He was to discover that many restaurants had small groups of musicians playing during meal time.

After tea he went to the cinema to see a film starring Rita Hayworth and Phil Silvers.

Antwerp was a great contrast to Nijmegen. Here they were far removed from the war and the people were returning to a peace time situation.

On the other side of the street from the Excelsior was the Century Hotel. The two hotels were linked by an underground passageway in which there were some rather expensive looking shops. The Century seemed to be the poshest hotel in Antwerp and only the most important visitors were housed there.

After the film Charlie had a look round Antwerp, a city he was to get to know quite well, later on.

Back in his hotel he had another bath and after a good night's sleep had a third bath before going down for breakfast.

Then he had to return to Nijmegen and the reality of war.

Communications between the forces seemed to be improving. Charlie remembers being called to a meeting to be informed, in secret, that the Americans had captured a bridge over the Rhine at Remagen. When he saw the Bergsma's he told them there was some good news but he wasn't allowed to reveal it yet. A few hours later they heard the news on the Dutch radio.

The Bergsma family spoke very good English and were well read. They introduced Charlie to the Forsyte Saga novels by John Galsworthy. They had a daughter, Hilda, who was attached to SHAEF the Supreme HQ of the Allied Expeditionary Forces. She acted as an interpreter and with her knowledge of Holland and Germany was very valuable to them. Charlie only met her once.

A lot of Dutch people had relations in Germany. In fact in one small town near Maastricht there was a railway crossing the main street. On one side of the street it was Holland and on the other side was Germany. It was not surprising that some Dutch people were in the German army and the Dutch S.S. troops were a very determined enemy.

On the 10th April, 1945 Charlie was briefed on the plan to capture Arnhem. 56 Brigade was to lead the attack by 49 Division. They were to seize the area just south of Arnhem. 146 Brigade would follow and cross the river, then 147 Brigade would go through and seize the high ground north of Arnhem. Assault craft were to be used to cross the river and the Royal Engineers were to construct a pontoon bridge. There was to be bomber support. Six field regiments of heavy artillery were involved as well as two heavy A.A.batteries and two regiments of LAA (Bofors 40m.m.) guns of which 89 LAA regiment was one.

The Canadian army were to cross the Neder Rhine to the west of 49 division and the British troops of the Second Army had already crossed the Rhine in the east as had the Americans.

Arnhem was finally captured on 15th April, 1945. The German forces withdrew towards Germany but the Dutch SS continued to fight the Canadians.

Arnhem had obviously been a pretty town with its avenues of trees on the main roads. It had taken seven months since the operation 'Market Garden' started until its final capture. Those houses that had not been destroyed by bombing or shelling had been systematically looted and the interiors destroyed by the Germans as an act of revenge.

89 LAA Regiment finished up in an area between Appeldoorn and Utrecht. There had been a great food shortage during the last months of the German occupation and the Dutch people north of the Neder Rhine were literally starving.

On 4th May, 1945 the German forces in Holland, Denmark and Western Germany surrendered to General Montgomery at Luneberg Heath. The previous evening when it was known that the surrender was to take place, the Canadian soldiers just north of 89 LAA Regiment started firing all their weapons into the air, not considering where all the shells and bullets were landing back on earth. It was time to take cover.

Chapter 20

The 8th May was VE day, VE meaning victory in Europe. Everyone in Britain was having a day's holiday. There were street parties everywhere. The King and Queen stood on the balcony of Buckingham Palace with Winston Churchill and the two princesses as thousands stood outside cheering the victory. All over liberated Europe there were celebrations but Charlie, with a small group, was detailed to spend the day making sure that nobody came on to a gunnery firing range near the German border. The war against Japan had to be won and it was necessary that the field gunners start preparing to go to the Far East.

When he returned to battery HQ he found everyone in a very relaxed mood. Someone had presented them with a carboy of Dutch gin. Unfortunately, no-one was very keen on the taste. The exception was Major 'John'. One evening when everyone had gone to bed, John was still in the officers' mess drinking his gin. In the morning when the kitchen staff came in, John was fast asleep in a chair. When he awoke he went to his room to wash and shave and change clothes before coming down to breakfast. After breakfast he decided to go with his batman driver, Davies, to see some troops in Utrecht. He insisted on driving. They sped along this straight road which ran parallel to a canal. They came to a bend in the road and in the canal. John was too late in braking. Davies jumped out of the Jeep onto the grass verge. The Jeep went straight into the canal.

Davies, recounting the event said, "There was a great splash and a large bubble of air arose to the surface". Inside was Major John, who said on surfacing, "Are you alright Davies?"

Davies walked along the road to find a lorry with lifting tackle to pull the Jeep out of the canal. When he got back there was no sign of John. After a search he was found fast asleep under a hedge.

ALIAS CHARLIE

With the defeat of Germany the process of demobilisation started. According to one's age and length of service, men were allotted a number. Since Charlie was still young but had been almost six years in the army his demob number was 26. The people with the lowest number were demobilised first. With the number 26 is wasn't expected that Charlie would be sent to the Far East but there was an officer whose father held a high position in the Conservative party, he managed to get a lift back to England on an RAF plane to make sure he wouldn't go East.

Life in Holland started to get back to normality. Food supplies were rushed in, just in time for many of the inhabitants. The Germans had commandeered most of the cattle. Some enterprising Canadians started driving lorries into Germany removing beasts from the German farms then selling the cattle to Dutch farmers. The practice was illegal but some Canadians became quite wealthy as a result.

Shortly afterwards 46 Division moved into the Ruhr Valley. All along the road every building seemed to have been destroyed. People were living like rats amongst the ruins. There was a great shortage of food. Charlie's battery finished up in Bochum. The Americans had conquered the area and stripped it of anything worth having, although Charlie did manage to get a couple of cameras from the Rathaus (the Town Hall)

British soldiers had been ordered not to fraternise with the Germans and this was observed in the main. However, British soldiers didn't like to see the young children starving and regularly gave them their sweets and biscuits.

The Ruhr Valley was the industrial heartland of Germany and Russian and Polish civilians and captured soldiers were forced to work in the mines and factories.

Charlie was given responsibility to look after one camp. There were 250 Russian men, women and children in the camp none of whom spoke any English. There was, however, a Serb who could speak some French and Charlie's limited French skills were severely tested.

The leader of the camp was a Russian civilian with no real authority. The first thing they required was a large iron pot in which they could cook their food. One was eventually found in a factory and was set up in the camp. Each day the ration lorry would come to deliver their food. All the rations went into the boiler to be cooked and served out twice a day. Meat, jam, potatoes, vegetables, bread, powdered milk and so on went into the stew. It was said that when delousing powder was sent out that also went into the stew.

Some of the men in the camp lazed about all day then slipped out of the back of the camp at night to go and rob Germans. Some of the German people claimed they had been threatened with guns.

One day Charlie and his sergeant went into the camp to search for guns. They explained to the camp leader what they were going to do. He and the Serb went with them to look into every nook and cranny. In each hut they found sacks of black hard bread being stored under the beds. This was rye bread which they would take back to Russia. They knew that life would be hard when they got back and the rye bread would help to prevent starvation.

As they proceeded round the camp the rest of the residents followed, looking into everything that the search party had seen.

Eventually a hand gun and some ammunition were found hidden in the chimney of a stove. The men in that hut were arrested and sent to a Russian officers' camp to be punished. The next day they were back at the camp.

There was a 10 p.m. curfew which meant that everyone had to be off the streets by then. It was difficult to enforce the curfew when bus loads and lorry loads of people were making their way back to their native countries. Italians, French, Dutch, Belgians and various other groups who had been made to work for the Germans were desperately trying to get back home. Some were going South, others were going North. It was amazing how many displaced people there were.

Charlie took his share of night time patrols with soldiers to try to make sure that things were kept as peaceful as possible.

In many ways it was an unrealistic world but then the whole war period was full of abnormal happenings.

Chapter 21

There were two other camps where Charlie had some measure of responsiblity. One was a camp of Russian officers who had been taken prisoner. They were totally different from the peasants in the other camp. They had regular meals where the different items of food were cooked properly. The senior officer was a major. Charlie had a meeting with him and some of the other officers to make some arrangements. When they seemed to have reached a decision it was countermanded by someone who seemed to have no military rank.. Charlie surmised that he was probably a member of OGPU the secret police.

The third camp contained Polish soldiers and civilians. This camp was bigger than the other two and seemed to be better informed as to what was happening in Eastern Europe. Here the camp leader was a brigadier. They were a very friendly group and Charlie remembers being invited to a dance there. When it became time for the various nationalities to go back home, the Poles in this camp refused to go. There was no way they would return to a Poland under Russian control.

One day Charlie was required to go with a Russian officer to a Geman coal mine. The mine was a revelation to him. It was so different to the mine in Scotland which he had visited in his student days. There was this vast hall with pulleys high up. As a miner came off shift he would have a shower, his working clothes would go up on his pulley and his walking out clothes would come down. These German miners went home clean unlike the miners in Scotland.

The Russian officer went round asking questions from all sorts of people but he was unable to find the man he was looking for.

One night Charlie and two other officers were invited to dinner at a hospital for Russian soldiers which was being run by Russian doctors. The meal started at 10 p.m. Charlie was the senior of the three British officers. As such he sat beside the senior Russian who was a major. They were served with slices of meat on a plate and a glass of brandy. A toast was proposed to the victory. The Russian major insisted that Charlie empty his glass and turn it over to prove that it was empty. More meat was served and more brandy. The toast was to Marshal Stalin. Again more meat, more brandy and a toast to Winston Churchill. The procedure was repeated during the two hours of the meal in which toasts had been drunk to all the Russian, British and American generals. Towards the end the Russian major had stopped turning his glass over. When they left Charlie felt light headed but not drunk. The slices of meat seemed to have absorbed the brandy.

When it was time for the Russian peasants to return by train to Russia, the Serb who had been Charlie's interpreter begged not to be sent back. He feared he would be shot. Charlie assured him that he wouldn't be and wrote him a letter to take with him saying how helpful he had been. It was only in later years that Charlie learned how returning refugees were treated. His letter would be like a death sentence. It is to be hoped he was able to get off that train before it got to Russia.

While Charlie was in the Ruhr Valley he and his batman driver, Sam George, took the opportunity to visit the Mohne Dam, the walls of which were breached in May 1943 by the 'Dambuster' squadron led by Wing Commander Guy Gibson. The bouncing bombs developed by Barnes Wallis had to be dropped very precisely from a height of 60 feet. Each bomb weighed five tons. When released the bombs bounced along the surface until they hit the wall where they sank and exploded. The bombs tore a huge hole in the wall. The water went rushing down the Ruhr Valley destroying power supplies and factories producing war weapons.

It was certainly a set back for the Germans but at what a cost. Eight Lancaster bombers were lost and fifty three crew died. It was no wonder that Barnes Wallis regretted having designed the bomb.

Charlie and Sam travelled along the wide road which was on

the top of the repaired wall. Charlie still has photos he took of Sam sitting on the edge of the wall.

Other dams were attacked in the raid but the destruction of the Mohne Dam was the main target and the main success.

Chapter 22

While in Germany 89 LAA Regiment set up a little holiday hotel on the Zuider Zee in Holland to which officers could go for a little break. Charlie and a friend Jim went for a couple of days beside the sea. The hotel had some stables and there were horses that had been captured from the Germans. One afternoon Charlie went along to see if he could have a horse to ride. The only horse available was one that hadn't been ridden for a month because of a foot injury.

Charlie had never ridden a horse before but he confidently mounted the animal and after some persuasion it started off. They were proceeding quite gently along the road when they approached an open railway crossing. Coming towards them was a Churchill tank and along the line a train was approaching. The poor horse took fright and started to bolt along a path beside the railway. Charlie didn't know what to do for the best, hold on grimly or get off quickly.

As they sped along they passed a group of soldiers who started cheering and shouting, "Come on Steve", Steve Donoghue being the most successful pre-war jockey.

Eventually the horse slowed up and Charlie was able to guide it back to the stables. Charlie made a resolution not to go riding again until he'd had some lessons.

Reflecting on this ride reminded him of the brilliant poem, "The Diverting History of John Gilpin", written by William Cowper (1731–1800).

> "So, Fair and softly", John he cried,
> But John he cried in vain,
> That trot became a gallop soon,
> In spite of curb and rein.

ALIAS CHARLIE

So stooping down, as needs he must
Who cannot sit upright
He grasped the mane with both his hands,
And eke with all his might.

His horse, who never in that sort
Had handled been before,
What thing upon his back had got
Did wonder more and more.

Away went Gilpin, neck or nought,
Away went hat and wig;
He little dreamt, when he set out,
Of running such a rig!

The dogs did bark, the children screamed,
Up flew the windows all;
And every soul cried out; 'Well done!'
As loud as he could bawl.

Whenever he sees jockeys riding racehorses, Charlie knows that he could never have become a jockey. Sitting on such powerful beasts is a very precarious business and why anyone wants to ride a horse in the Grand National is beyond him.

Now that the war in Europe was over it was time to start losing weapons. Charlie was directed to take a troop of six Bofors guns to a depot in Antwerp. Each Bofors gun was towed by a lorry. They made good progress through Germany, Holland and Belgium before deciding to stop for the night at Herentals. This would leave them with a short journey to Antwerp the following morning.

The next morning as they got into the city the drivers bunched up closer to each other. They came to a sudden stop. One driver was not quick enough applying his brakes. His windscreen smashed into the muzzle of a Bofors gun. Fortunately, no one was hurt but the windscreen was shattered. Charlie was annoyed to think they had come all that long way just to have this happen in the last few miles. He wondered what would be said when they handed the lorries and guns in. He needn't have worried. He was told where to leave the lorries and guns in this large park where they would wait before being returned to the UK.

They now had only one lorry, the one that Charlie had been travelling in. This would take them all back to Germany. He and the drivers decided to stay in Antwerp for the night. The only problem was money. They had no Belgian currency. They were able to change some of their German marks into Belgian francs but not enough for a real spree. Charlie booked himself in at the Excelsior Hotel.

It was nice to be back in Antwerp. He went to a local bar where he met some other officers. One of them gave him some Belgian money in exchange for a cheque.

The following day they returned to the Ruhr without incident. They could travel back much more quickly now that they hadn't to tow guns and travel in convoy.

About this time Charlie had his first leave back to England. It was great to be back home with Hilda and baby Susan even if it was only for a week. Charlie found himself fearful of walking on grass verges. In Europe so many mines had been laid in verges that you had to be very careful where you walked. Instinctively, back in Doncaster he found himself afraid of walking on to a mine.

The leave passed all too quickly but at least the war in Europe was over and he would be released from the Army in due time.

Chapter 23

When Charlie was at university he wondered what he should try to do after he left. The Metropolitan Police had a scheme whereby athletic young graduates could go to Hendon Police College. If they completed the course satisfactorily then after two years they would leave with the rank of Junior Inspector which would lead to accelerated promotion to higher ranks. This idea appealed to him and he intended to apply once he'd got his degree.

After he had been in the army for a year he thought he might go back to university to train to be a doctor. When he got married and had a baby daughter that wasn't feasible. The Hendon Police College scheme had ended thus teaching became the most obvious career to aim for.

With so many soldiers waiting to be demobilised it was decided that educational units should be set up in each regiment or battalion to help soldiers prepare for return to civilian life. The Army Educational Corps was greatly expanded and Charlie applied to join the AEC.

On 25th June, 1945 he went for interview to the Education Branch at the HQ of 21st Army Group which was stationed in Wentworth Barracks in Herford, Germany.

Here again chance came in to favour him. In England an M.A. degree was a higher degree but in Scotland it was an ordinary degree. The English major who interviewed him didn't know that and thought Charlie was more qualified than he was.

Charlie was told that he would be informed, in due course, of the result of the interview.

About two weeks later he was posted to join the Army Education Corps at 21 Army Group HQ. The major who had interviewed him had organised a course for officers and sergeants and he wanted Charlie to assist him.

On the morning of the 6th August, 1945 news came over the radio that a new type of bomb, an atomic bomb, had been dropped on the thriving city of Hiroshima. The bomb was so powerful that it destroyed the whole city.

At first Charlie was inclined to think this was just a piece of propaganda. When he had been at university there was no knowledge of atoms splitting like this. Talking to a young sergeant who had recently been at university, he was told about the structure within the atom. He realised that a lot had happened in the world of physics during the seven years since he had studied the subject.

Three days after the bomb on Hiroshima a second atomic bomb was dropped on the port of Nagasaki. The first bomb had been a uranium 235 bomb. The second was a plutonium bomb.

In later years many people have queried whether it was right to drop these bombs on civilians. At the time most people felt that it was the only way to bring Japan to its knees quickly. There were so many allied soldiers, sailors, airmen and civilians living in the most brutal conditions in Japanese camps that the sooner they were released, the better.

On the 14th August Emperor Hirohito announced the Japanese surrender and on 2nd September the surrender document was signed aboard the USS Missouri in Tokyo Bay.

In 1964 Charlie wrote a book, called "The Story of the Atom", which outlined how knowledge had developed about the nature of the structure of the atoms. The story was not published although material from the book was used by Blackies as the basis of a book by another author.

Chapter 24 is a reproduction of the first chapter in his book.

Chapter 24

Hiroshima

Farm Hall, a large brick built house near Godmanchester in Huntingdonshire, was the temporary prison of the ten top German atomic scientists during August 1945. Why these scientists were being held there was not quite clear to them. They knew that it had something to do with the fact that they were nuclear physicists. What they did not know was that the scientists of Britain, Canada and the USA had been working together for years to produce an atomic bomb in the belief that the Germans had started on this work before them. The fear that Hitler might at any time have the use of such a weapon was the spur that had caused engineers and scientists to forget their scruples and set about the work of producing the bomb before the Germans.

Before the war Gottingen University, in Germany had been the foremost centre for the study of theoretical mathematics and physics. It was here in this peaceful little town that many of the ideas with regard to the structure of atoms had first been discussed. At the start of the war these German scientists knew as much as any group of scientists about the terrific power locked in the nucleus of atoms. They were well placed to lead the world in the manufacture of atomic weapons if that had been their wish.

Fortunately that had not been their wish. Many of them were not prepared to cooperate fully with the Nazi Party of Hitler. They all thought, in any case, that the problems of producing an atomic bomb were too formidable to undertake during a war. It is likely that the same thing would have happened in America but for the thought that the Germans were already working under Hitler's orders to produce such a weapon.

The ten scientists had been collected and brought to Britain by a special unit of the American army which had been given this task as the Allied armies fought their way through Germany. It was with relief that the leaders of this unit discovered the little progress that had been made by the Germans. When the scientists were arrested they were sent to Britain until someone could decide what should be done with them.

On the 6th August, 1945 an American plane dropped an atomic bomb on the Japanese city of Hiroshima. The German scientists could hardly believe the news. They were sure it was some propaganda trick until the details of the damage done was given on the nine o' clock news by the BBC. They were dumbfounded. How could their scientific friends produce such a bomb? Why had it been dropped? How could they possibly overcome all the technical difficulties? Argument raged fierce amongst them.

The younger scientists blamed the older ones for not having made enough effort for the cause of Germany. The older scientists were perplexed and saddened.

In the peaceful days before Hitler, scientists from all over the world had come to the sleepy little town of Gottingen to share their ideas. In those days they had all been friends sharing a common interest, the new fascinating knowledge about the structure of atoms. The rise of Hitler had changed this. First the German Jews had been forced to flee from the Nazis. They had gone wherever they could find refuge. Many went to Britain, more to the USA and some to Denmark. In place of friendship there was suspicion and hostility. It was this very suspicion that hastened the development of the atomic bomb.

These older Germans had taken their share in producing the new ideas which had seemed so wonderful and harmless. Otto Hahn, the discoverer of nuclear fission, was particularly disturbed. The thought that inadvertently he had helped to produce a bomb which had destroyed a city of 200,000 people was too much to bear. Suicide seemed to be the only way out. But the others seeing the effect that the news had on him kept a close watch to see that he did not take this course.

If these ten Germans were depressed by the news, the people of Britain and America were overjoyed. The war against Germany had just ended but there were prospects of bitter fighting before the Japanese would finally be beaten. The Japanese had committed so many atrocities that little sympathy was felt for them. They were only getting a taste of their own medicine.

What of the scientists who had helped to make the bomb? Here there was a mixture of emotions; pride that the bomb had done what it had been designed to do but also regret that the bomb had been dropped. A few weeks earlier the first bomb had been tested at Alamogordo in the American desert of New Mexico. The successful explosion had shown that this was a terrible new weapon. Many of the scientists had signed a petition addressed to President Truman of the USA to ask that a demonstration of the power of the bomb be given to observers from all over the world, including the Japanese, to show what would happen to Japan if she did not capitulate.

The advisers of the President thought that this would not produce the required result and so the bomb was dropped. Many of those who had given all their effort to produce it were horrified. They felt that at the least some warning should have been given to the Japanese beforehand, especially about the hazards of the radiation which would be produced when the bomb exploded. Many were vexed that the weapon had been used not on a military target but on a defenceless city. They felt that they had been betrayed. They had worked on the bomb in the belief that Hitler's scientists had started on it before them. When it was known that, in fact, Germany had made little progress on it there was no longer any justification for having it and certainly no right to use it.

The Russians too were none too pleased by the news. Although Britain, America and Russia were allies there had been no cooperation between them on atomic weapons. The Russians had been denied all knowledge of the progress that had been made.

It has been said that the atomic bomb was not only the last bomb of the Second World War but the first of the Cold War. Certainly the fact that Russia had been excluded from this knowledge was not going to make for a closer relationship between East and West.

The leaders of Japan were also completely surprised by the news of the atom bomb. The first reports they received, said that Hiroshima had been completely destroyed by two bombers. Later they learned that one bomb only had been dropped. They had to wait for the news from America to learn that it was an atomic bomb. This meant nothing to them so they sent for their leading atomic scientist Yoshio Nishina to ask him if such a bomb were possible. When he had heard the details he was considerably shaken but affirmed that the only kind of bomb that could produce this sort of damage would be an atomic bomb. He was then asked if there was any defence against such a bomb. To this he replied that the only defence would be to shoot down every American bomber before it reached Japan. This the Japanese realised was impossible. He was then asked whether Japan could produce such a bomb within six months for it was felt that they could hold out for that length of time. Nishina replied that there was no possibility of Japan being able to make one for several years.

They had no supply of uranium and there was not enough technical knowledge available in the country.

The leaders still found it hard to realise that this was the end. Nishina volunteered to fly to Hiroshima to report on the power of the bomb. When he flew over the devastated city he realised that indeed only one bomb had been dropped. He could see where it had landed and the ruins spreading out for miles around.

He was met at the airport by the officer in charge. One half of his face was badly burned. The other side was undamaged. He was not very worried about the burns for he had no idea that he had received a massive dose of radiation.

Ninety thousand people were killed immediately the bomb fell on Hiroshima. Tens of thousands more died later as the effects of radiation burns destroyed the cells of their bodies.

On the 9th August, 1945 a second atomic bomb was dropped on Japan. This failed to explode in the air as had been intended but even so the town of Nagasaki was obliterated. On the 15th August Japan surrendered unconditionally.

The war had been won, but at what cost. Tens of millions of people had died as a result of it. Every country taking part had been impoverished and now a terrible new weapon had been constructed. From now on the people of the world were to live under a cloud, a cloud of instant death.

Chapter 25

Two weeks after the Japanese surrender Charlie was promoted to captain and sent to join a brigade of the 15th Scottish Division as Brigade Education Officer. The brigade HQ was stationed in a small village north of Hamburg. The officers had taken over a beautiful rest home and were quartered there. In the village a rather nice house was serving as the Education Centre. When Charlie arrived it was being run by four sergeants who seemed to have everything under control.

Charlie's role was to liaise with the battalion education officers and those in the other brigades and at divisional HQ.

Soldiers were brought together to have talks on two subjects. One week the subject was Current Affairs. The other week the study was on the British Constitution and matters relating to government. Booklets were provided on both subjects. The basic idea was that all soldiers should know what was going on in the world around them.

Charlie's visits to other units were more social than educational. He would be invited into the officers' mess for a drink and a lunch. Likewise he would entertain officers from other units.

The brigadier, Dick Villiers, was very friendly as were all the other officers. Charlie was asked if he could play bridge and when he said he had played a little, found that he was to be the brigadier's partner for the games which were played most evenings after dinner

He was also expected to accompany the brigadier if he wanted to see a film or a show. One film they went to see was Wuthering Heights. On another occasion a touring ENSA party was giving a show in a nearby theatre. The star of the show was Gertrude Lawrence who starred in the musicals written by Noel Coward. In those days she had been every young man's dream girl. After the show she and the cast came out to talk to people. Charlie asked the brigadier if he would like to be introduced to her. The brigadier shook his head. He was disappointed to see how she looked now. In his mind's eye he thought she'd still look like the young beauty whom he'd seen in his youth.

One night they had a party when the general commanding 15th Scottish Division was invited. A piper played them into dinner. When he had finished he was given a large glass of whisky. After dinner the piper played the music for an eightsome reel in which they all took part even though there were no women there.

The general was a a very tall man well over six feet tall and was nicknamed 'Tiny' Barbour. The other brigadiers in the division were also invited and Charlie found himself playing a game of 'Pokey Die' with a general and four brigadiers. The game was played with four dice which were hidden and passed round. Each player had to improve on the statement of the person before. The first player might say there were two jacks, the next would say 'two jacks and a queen'. The game was highly competitive and they were each trying to put one over on the others. Charlie wasn't really involved.

One of Charlie's sergeants was a Jew. He seemed to get rather a lot of mail. It was only in later years that Charlie realised that he was being used to pass on letters to other Jews some of whom were trying to get into Israel.

On a Saturday afternoon Charlie often went into Hamburg. There was a very big officers' club in an hotel on the lakeside. There he sometimes met officers whom he'd known well who were in other units.

Often he would go to the concert hall where the Hamburg State Orchestra would be playing music which was being broadcast live on the radio. It was here and in the Brigade mess that he developed a fondness for Beethoven's symphonies. In the Brigade mess there was a very good wind up gramophone and a stack of records. The music was mainly German, Mozart, Beethoven and Wagner.

In the education centre they often had little recitals and talks about composers and their music. They had a grand piano and many fine pianists came to play there.

Each education centre was provided with a library of books. The various publishers allowed the forces to have them on the understanding that they would not be sold but be handed back and destroyed.

It was in this library that Charlie read the book, "Three Men in a Boat", by Jerome K. Jerome. It was the most humorous book he'd ever read. The dog Montmorency was a little terrier and was so like others he knew, a real troublemaker.

Another book which was a best seller was 'Mathematics for the Million' by Lancelot Hogben. The aim of the book was to make non mathematicians interested in the subject. It showed how mathematics developed from the earliest times. He followed this book with 'Science for the Citizen' which was also a best seller.

In December 1945 Charlie was given a week's leave to go home to Doncaster. Hilda had been negotiating for them to buy a house. The asking price was £700 which Hilda's family thought was too much since it had only cost £350 to build. When they sold it two years later, it fetched £1,450, so it turned out to be a very profitable purchase.

A cash deposit of £50 was required so Charlie went to the Midland Bank to receive ten £5 notes which he took to the solicitor who was handling the sale. When Charlie had returned to Germany it was found that one of the notes was counterfeit. it was assumed that Charlie had brought it over from Germany. Fortunately, when Hilda checked with the bank they agreed that they'd given him the note. In those days a £5 note was worth more than £100 now and the bank kept a note of the numbers of all the fivers they handled.

Back in Germany in January the weather was very cold. The brigadier was quite a good skater and all the officers had a go at skating on this large frozen lake. Charlie never really got the hang of it.

He began to feel ill. The doctor examined him and suggested he spend a few days in bed. He gave Charlie some ascorbic acid pills saying that the lack of vitamin C was the cause of the illness. In retrospect Charlie is sure it was a mild attack of rheumatic fever, an illness he was to get again in 1949.

ALIAS CHARLIE

During his time near Hamburg he went to a three day conference in Lubeck on the Baltic Sea. The war seemed to have bypassed this city. In the harbour were many tall sailing ships. Charlie thought it was a really beautiful city.

At the conference was an infantry colonel who had been wounded in Normandy and had just returned to his battalion. In the officers' mess a gin and tonic cost sixpence and he thought this was marvellously cheap. He enjoyed the luxury of more than a few drinks at this price.

The Chief Education Officer for Hertfordshire came out to talk to people who were thinking of becoming teachers. Teaching could be a fulfilling job. There wouldn't be much jam but you could be sure of your bread and butter.

Chapter 26

Shortly afterwards Charlie and another officer got the chance to go to Copenhagen for a 48 hour leave. It was quite a long drive through Denmark and on to the island where Copenhagen is situated. They had been told that the rate of exchange was such that British money did not buy much. They were only allowed to spend £15 each (about £300 now). To help pay for their board and visits it was suggested they take as many cigarettes as they could gather to help buy what they wanted.

The young man in charge of the Church of Scotland mobile canteen gave Charlie 600 cigarettes to buy him a wrist watch in Denmark.

When Dave and Charlie got to Copenhagen they went to the Town Major's office to be allocated to an hotel. They were in there for about ten minutes but when they came out and got into their Jeep they found that all their cigarettes had been stolen.

They went to their hotel wondering how they were going to be able to manage. Someone told them that if they went to a British Army petrol station they could get a jerrycan of petrol, about four gallons, for the return journey. They could then take it to a back street Danish garage where it would sell for a good price. This they did. They now had enough money to do what they wanted.

Throughout Europe money was never good currency. Cigarettes and chocolate were of more value. In Germany Charlie got a hand made leather briefcase for a packet of 20 cigarettes.

In Britain as in Europe, there was a 'black market'. Certain people were able to get hold of things which were in very short supply and sell them in a most profitable way. It was the era of the spiv.

In Belgium the government decided to change its currency. The new Belgian franc could be got for ten old francs by going to your bank. However, there was a limit as to how much you could change and beyond that you had to be able to prove that you had gained the money honestly. Many 'spivs' and farmers found they had lots of old francs which they couldn't use.

Soldiers on leave in Antwerp were allowed to change one old franc for one new franc within a certain limit. Charlie was on leave in Antwerp when he was approached by the officer who'd been able to fly back to England to make sure he wasn't posted to the Far East. He asked Charlie to change some old francs for him. Apparently, he was buying old francs from farmers at a very cheap rate then getting softies, like Charlie, to take them to the bank in exchange for new francs.

In England in 1957, Hilda and Charlie were selling their home near Beverley, he having been promoted to a new post in another town. The house was up for sale at £2,500. A lady who had had a shop in Beverley throughout the war offered to buy the house for £1,000 and hand over the other £1,500 in cash. Charlie explained to her that they could not sell a house for a nominal £1,000 when they had a mortgage of £2,000.

She had made so much money in the black market that she couldn't put it into the bank and of course she hadn't paid income tax on this money.

When they lived in Doncaster, Hilda sent Charlie into the open air market to do some shopping. He had an old 'sit up and beg' bicycle, the kind that policemen used to ride pre-war. He went up to this stallholder and asked if he had any nylons for sale. The stallholder suspecting that Charlie was a policeman produced a pair of nylon stockings which Hilda was delighted to receive.

On another day he was sent to buy some fish. Meat was rationed but fish wasn't. In the fishmongers he saw some steaks of whale meat. He thought he would buy that instead of fish. Hilda wasn't too pleased with him, particularly after she'd cooked the steaks. They looked like beefsteaks but tasted like fish.

Throughout the war, bread had never been rationed, but a year or so after the end of the war, the Attlee government brought in bread rationing, much to the disgust of the British people. What they did not know, was that Earl Mountbatten, who was Governor

General of India, had informed Attlee that India was suffering from a great grain shortage and many people were starving.

Attlee decided to divert some ships which were carrying wheat from Canada to Britain, to go to India instead and to introduce bread rationing in Britain.

This only came to light many years later when AJP Taylor, the Oxford historian, revealed it in one of his radio broadcasts.

The fact that Clement Attlee was prime minister rather than Winston Churchill was the surprise of the first peace time general election. The forces' vote was very heavily in favour of Labour. Churchill was greatly admired as a war leader but the forces wanted a country which gave the ordinary person a better deal that they'd had pre-war.

In 1944 Rab Butler the Conservative Minister for Education brought in a new act to improve educational opportunities after the war.

The main thing that the new Labour government did was to introduce the National Health Service which provided for free health care for everyone.

Charlie's sister, Anne, married a doctor. When Hilda, Charlie and the children visited them just after the war, Dr. John would come back from visits to patients with his pockets full of half crowns. He would empty all this money into a big brass bowl. Anyone needing money could help themselves from the bowl.

There were some arrangements whereby certain workmen were 'on the panel' but for most people a visit from the doctor was very costly as was a visit to the dentist.

In Clydebank a new council estate was being built. Two enterprising newly qualified doctors set up a practice in a double decker bus in the centre of the estate. The downstairs was the waiting room and the upstairs was the surgery. As the estate grew so did the number of their patients so that when a new health centre was opened they already had a large number of patients on their list.

Chapter 27

In March 1946, Charlie had another week's leave back in the UK. Hilda and Susan were now well established in their new house in Doncaster and as a result of the December leave Hilda was again pregnant.

Furniture was the big problem. When you set up home you were given some dockets which allowed you to buy some furniture but the shops were empty and you had to wait several months after you'd given your dockets to the shop before the furniture would arrive. The new furniture was called 'utility' furniture. In other words it was cheaply made but at least it was furniture. Hilda had been going to auction sales and second hand shops to see what she could find. Their first dressing table consisted of two orange boxes covered with a cloth with a portable mirror on top.

They had a double bed and a cot for Susan but very little else. However, they were happy to be setting up home and they knew Charlie would soon be demobilised.

When he got back to Hamburg he found that the brigade had been disbanded. There was a skeleton staff remaining to sort out problems, but most had gone back to the UK.

There were instructions for Charlie to go to Antwerp to take up a post as education officer there. He'd had a large wooden chest made for him and inside he put all the things he was no longer likely to use and had it sent to Hilda.

He was able to get all he needed into his valise and a haversack. Then he caught the train in Hamburg to go on the long slow journey to Antwerp. He found out that the train was due to stop in Nijmegen so on the spur of the moment he decided to call and see the Bergma family. He got to their house just before they were due to go to Amsterdam in a hired cab. They were going to see friends whom they hadn't been able to see for a long time. They invited Charlie to go with them.

It was interesting to see Amsterdam, the city with all the canals. They travelled back in the evening. Charlie stayed the night in Nijmegen then caught the train to Antwerp the next morning.

The set up in Antwerp was very much in the control of four sergeants. Charlie was installed in a modern flat in the centre of town. He doesn't remember doing much work there. The situation was very fluid. Units were being disbanded and men were returning to Britain to be demobbed. Three of the sergeants were talented musicians and they often practised together and Charlie often stopped to listen to them.

Charlie contacted Jean De Cooman, a solicitor, who had been second in command of the Belgian battalion which was part of Bobforce. He was made very welcome and invited to have evening meals with Jean and his wife.

He also took a train journey to Berlaar where he had stayed with Louis De Kock Meulders, his wife and two young sons. They gave him a great welcome too. Louis had written to Hilda anxious to know how Charlie was getting on after he had left their home.

Charlie kept in contact with the De Coomans and the De Kock Meulders for the next 30 years. In 1970 Mrs Bergma came to England on a music course and stayed with Charlie and Hilda for three days.

Three weeks after settling in Antwerp, he went on a two week course to Gottingen University. There was a wide choice of courses and Charlie chose to do a refresher course on mathematics.

Gottingen was another town which didn't seem to have been much affected by the war. The facilities at the university were excellent, much better than at Glasgow University.

Charlie struck up a friendship with a captain from Glasgow who had been operating behind enemy lines in a unit known as 'Phantom' In peace time he was a graphic designer working for a large store in Glasgow.

There was an indoor riding school in Gottingen and they went along to try out their riding skills. Riding with just your toes in the stirrups and going round in small circles and figures of eight was not very comfortable for Charlie. After two lessons he decided horse riding was not going to be one of his skills.

There was a beautiful opera house in Gottingen and Charlie managed to see a splendid performance of 'Carmen'.

After the course he went back to Antwerp to say goodbye to his friends then back to Britain to go through the demobilisation process on 10th April 1946.

Chapter 28

After Hilda's death in November 1998, I found myself with a lot of time on my hands. The past few years had been fully occupied helping Hilda as she progressively became more ill. So much of my time had been taken up hospital visiting.

One Wednesday afternoon I saw a notice in Redcar Library saying that Redcar Writers' Club was meeting in the library at 7 p.m. that night.

I decided to go along to see what it was like. There were a few people there and Brian Morton, the leader of the group, spoke about the things to think about when writing a short story.

I thought I would try my hand and wrote a story about my time in the peacetime Militia. Since my nickname in the Militia was Lofty, I used this as the title and Charlie Greene was the name I gave myself.

Having written the story I found that I enjoyed spending an hour or two writing at night, TV being very boring. It helped to pass the time and brought back many distant memories.

Now that Charlie Greene is about to leave the army I've decided to discard that name and use my own name, Bob Stirling, for the remainder of my story. When I was with the Sherwood Foresters, John Widgery always called me 'Bomber' because of the Stirling bomber then in use.

I arrived at Strensall Barracks in York on the evening of 9th April along with many others of all ranks who were to be demobbed. On arrival our names were ticked off the lists by the reception staff. We were given accommodation and an evening meal.

In the morning, after breakfast, we went into the large hall to select civilian clothing. I chose a blue suit with a white pin stripe, a pair of black shoes, a trilby hat, a shirt, socks and tie.

ALIAS CHARLIE

We donned our new clothes putting our uniforms in a parcel to carry home. I'd managed to send a telegram to Hilda to say I'd be arriving at Doncaster Station at 4.15 p.m on 10th April.

On my arrival I found Hilda and Susan waiting for me. It was a great feeling to back home at last. This was the day we had been yearning for, for such a long time. It was hard to believe that it had actually arrived.

The 10th April was the start of my demob. leave. On the 16th May I received the following letter from the War Office.

Sir,

Now that the time has come for your release from active military duty. I am commanded by the Army Council to express to you their thanks for the valuable services which you have rendered in the service of your country at a time of grave national emergency.

At the end of the emergency you will relinquish your commission, and at that time a notification will appear in the London Gazette (Supplement), granting you also the honorary rank of Captain. Meanwhile, you have permission to use that rank with effect from the date of your release.

I am, Sir,

Your obedient servant,

Eric BB Speed
Captain R Stirling,
Army Educational Corps.

Needless to say I didn't use the title in civvy street. The only person to use it was my mother who continued to address letters to Captain R Stirling, MA.

Now at home, Hilda and I decided to go on holiday with Susan to Swanage in Dorset. The beaches had been cleared of mines and the coils of barbed wire removed. It was back to being a quiet beauty spot in a lovely bay. We stayed at a little hotel which the owners had recently taken over from the Army. They were in the process of redecorating. One of their joys was to find 200 toilet rolls in a big cupboard. That would keep them going for a while.

When we were back home I had to find a job. I applied for a job with Doncaster Education Authority. The director of Education interviewed me. He told me that although technically, as a graduate, I was qualified to teach he would not give me a permanent teaching post until I'd completed a post graduate certificate of education course.

I contacted a divisional office of the West Riding Education Authority and was sent to a boys' junior school near Doncaster. Unfortunately, I made a bad start by arriving late on my first day. The journey involved two bus trips and took much longer than I'd anticipated. The head and I took an instant dislike to each other. In morning assemblies all the boys had to salute him. Since this wasn't the army I thought this was stupid. One lunch time I went on to the playing field with some boys. There was a long jump pit and I had them practising long jumps. He came storming out and ignoring me reprimanded the boys for jumping into the pit because it was forbidden.

Each day he would spend an hour playing the piano in the hall. He never did any teaching.

My classroom was directly opposite his office and he button-holed me when I hadn't taken a music lesson which was on my class timetable. I explained that I didn't play the piano. He said we had to practice scales and sing songs from the song books. After a few doh, ray, me's I got the song books out of the cupboard and asked the boys which songs they knew. The only song in the book that they knew was the National Anthem. So we sang "God save the King". Then we sang it again, getting louder each time for the next 35 minutes.

He was in his office hearing us but he didn't come in. At the end of my second week I found myself transferred to another primary school nearer my home.

This was a mixed junior school with a much friendlier head. I began to realise that I wasn't really ready to teach in a permanent post so I applied to Sheffield University to go on a course for the Post Graduate Certificate of Education.

The staff in this new school were very friendly and helpful. My outstanding memory was of a trip with the whole school to Belle Vue Zoo in Manchester. There were four bus loads and eight staff. When we got there I decided to keep my class with me all of the time. Two of the woman teachers thought it was a great chance to go into Manchester to do some shopping. After all, the children would all be within the confines of the zoo and there were other members of staff to keep an eye on them.

At 5 p.m. we gathered at the buses ready to go home. There was one boy missing. He was from the class of one of the teachers who'd gone into Manchester.

A frantic search of the Zoo took place. We looked in every cage, in the pool, restaurant, toilets and in evey part of the grounds but he wasn't to be found. We had to get the other pupils home, so the police were notified and we set back to Doncaster.

The boy's teacher was in a terrible state. How was she going to explain to his parents that he'd gone missing?

The boy was found wandering on a road outside the zoo by the police. He'd gone out of one of the exits and had been unable to get back in. The police informed the Doncaster police that he was safe and had been put on a train to Doncaster in the care of the guard.

It was a lesson to be learnt. When you take a party of children anywhere, make sure you stay with them.

Chapter 29

On 5th June, 1946, I went for an interview to Sheffield University to learn about the Post Graduate Certificate of Education course.

Those candidates with a good Honours degtree were likely to go to grammar schools and were required to train in two subjects only.

Students like me with a general degree were more likely to go to less specialised schools and were expected to train in three subjects. I chose Maths., Physics and History.

Sheffield had been heavily bombed during the war and the Education Department was based in a terrace of houses.

To prepare for an influx of graduates from the Forces the previous intake had been put through a course concentrated to six months instead of a year.

In the event there were only twenty six of us, all males. Some of the lecturers had also come out of the forces so that we were treated as equals.

On the night of 15th September, Hilda realised that her baby was due to be born. We'd just gone to bed so we had to get dressed. Fortunately, the son of our next door neighbour had just come in after his late night shift as a bus conductor. I asked him to come in and stay, in case Susan awoke, while I got a taxi to take Hilda to the Maternity home.

The next morning when I rang the home they said that we had a baby son, whom we named Robert Gordon, but called him Robin throughout his childhood.

I started travelling by bus to university every day. After a time I got to know others who did the same journey. Coming home I often sat with a man who had been a naval officer but was now a schools advisor. He said that when he came out of the Navy and found these posts of schools advisors were being advertised he decided to use an old naval adage, "If you can't beat them, join them".

The bus journey from Sheffield to Doncaster was quite interesting. When I'd lived in Clydebank I carried a raincoat on most days. Here in Sheffield I'd find it raining but halfway to Doncaster the rain would stop and in Doncaster I rarely needed a raincoat. Doncaster was further away from the hills than Sheffield.

January 1947 was very cold and the snow lay deep in Wheatley Hills where we lived. Susan needed Wellingtons but there were none in the shops. Hilda put an advert in the local evening paper. No sooner had the paper come out than people started coming to bring Wellingtons for Susan. The first to arrive was a police inspector with a pair that fitted Susan and were almost brand new.

During this period Robin spent every day wrapped up in his pram in the back garden. There was no way a pram could be pushed in the deep snow.

When the weather improved and Hilda was attending to Robin, Susan got into the habit of wandering off and visiting neighbours. It was then that we decided to see if we could get her into nursery school. There was a nice nursery school as part of the local infant school. I went to see the headmistress who had taught Hilda in junior school. There was a long waiting list but two days later we received a letter saying that Susan could start on the following Monday.

Susan loved nursery school. She had one particular boy friend. They'd go into school together not even bothering to say goodbye to Hilda. They had their lunch in school and after lunch mattresses were brought out and they had a little sleep. Hilda, with Robin in the pram, would pick her up at 3 p.m.

At Sheffield we did a course on different types of schools and their development. The lecturer didn't have any direct experience of nursery schools so I told the groups how the day was arranged and all the different activities they did. In the final exams there was a choice of questions on offer. Every member of my group chose to answer the nursery school question based on my knowledge.

I enjoyed the course at Sheffield. The work was less demanding than that of the degree course and also I was older and more able to handle things.

As part of the course we had to go to teach under supervision. The first school I went to was a mixed junior school. I was to spend two weeks there. There were two staff rooms. The four men teachers used one room. They all belonged to the National Association of Schoolmasters, (NAS). The eight women teachers and the headmistress belonged to the National Union of Teachers (NUT).

Which union a teacher joined was usually dependent on the college attended. Most colleges were single sex, particularly those where you boarded. Most women were NUT and men were equally divided between the two unions. In later years, a small union the Union of Women Teachers joined with the NAS to form the NASUWT.

In those days a woman was paid four fifths of a man's salary and the NAS was particularly keen to keep this difference in being.

I found teaching a class of nine year old children to be quite difficult. The spread of ability in a class always provided a problem. Do you spend more time with the less able? Do you try to teach the whole class at a medium level? What do you do for the really bright children? This was a problem then and still is today.

The 1944 Education Act was introduced by RA Butler. It promoted the idea of different types of secondary school as distinct from all age schools which had been the custom in villages.

Three types of secondary school were to be created. The most able pupils would go to grammar schools. The next group would go to technical schools and the third group would go to secondary modern schools. Selection would be by exam usually at the age of eleven

The children going to secondary modern schools were expected to be taught practical subjects, needlework and cookery for girls, woodwork and metalwork for boys. They would not take any external exams and would leave school at fourteen.

Technical schools were mainly for boys. They would take a

foreigh language, usually French and pay particular attention to mathematics and science. They would sit external exams.

The grammar schools were expected to teach Latin and another language, usually French. They would take external exams and stay longer at school.

That was the general idea. In practice what happened depended on the availability of school buildings.

I did a four week practice at a technical school near Sheffield. My final teaching practice was to be four weeks in a secondary modern school in Rotherham. After a week I was transferred to Hyde Park Boys' School, in Doncaster for the next three weeks. It was then time for the final exams. I took my last exam on a Saturday morning, the 31st May. The following Monday, the 2nd June, I started permanent employment at Hyde Park School.

This was extremely helpful because not only was I earning money through June and July but I also received pay throughout the summer holidays.

The Director of Education had kept his promise to me.

Chapter 30

Hyde Park School was a very old school. There was a boys' school and a girls' school which were on the same site but quite separate with separate playgrounds. The boys' building was quite roomy. It had classrooms which had been designed for classes of 50 but the usual size was now 30. The school hall had wooden walls and a high wooden roof. I've never attended a school where the singing was so good. The structure of the hall lent resonance to the singing.

In June 1947 the school leaving age was fourteen but in September the age was raised to fifteen. There were eight secondary modern classes and one technical class. The technical class stayed for one year before going on to the technical college. There were two classes in each year, an A and a B class. For the first two periods of each day the boys were divided into sets for English and Maths according to ability. In my first year I was given the bottom sets in English and Maths. At first I thought this was demeaning. I was the only graduate teacher in the school. But later I came to realise that this was a most profitable learning experience for me. During the war children's schooling was below normal standards. Many men teachers had been conscripted into the forces and were replaced by part time teachers. In some cases the children only had half day schooling. There was a lack of continuity.

The Hyde Park catchment was an area of old houses. Many pupils lived in a primitive way at home. In fact, George Sever, the senior master used to allow pupils who had no hot water at home, to have a good wash before school started. One new teacher found himself in trouble when he told a boy that if he continued to behave like that he would finish up in prison. He didn't know that the boy's father and elder brother were both in prison.

ALIAS CHARLIE

In my bottom English set most of the boys could barely read. The same could be said about the Maths group. There were twin brothers Jack and Fred. Fred was cleverer than Jack but still was at the bottom set level. One Monday I was thrilled when Jack got all his sums right. I congratulated him. He said, "Them were easy, I go round with the coalman on Saturday mornings". The sums had been about sacks of coal. If they'd been about bags of sugar he probably wouldn't have done them right.

Hilda's sister, May, was married to Gilbert who was the woodwork teacher. His main problem was getting wood for his lessons. All the wood being produced was going to build the new houses that were so badly needed. Gilbert scrounged wood from any possible source. He even cut up old railway sleepers. The boys' playground was surrounded by a stone wall. At the far end were two large wooden gates which were opened when the coal lorry came to deliver fuel. The headmaster and Gilbert decided they needed this wood for lessons. The gates were removed and the wood cut up.

A few months later the authority's Clerk of Works came round to try and find out why the school was asking for new gates. It was explained to him that the gates had been removed during the war. Metal gates and railings were removed to help provide the metal required for war weapons. The Clerk of Works didn't know that the gates had been wooden.

I found myself teaching some elementary science, a little history and taking the boys to the swimming baths and to the playing fields. There was another science teacher who spent some time down at the school garden which was about half a mile away. He was an odd character, reputed to walk round Doncaster at night dressed in women's clothes. The head wanted rid of him. The opportunity came when it was found that he'd been giving boys cigarettes and making improper suggestions.

In my second year, the technical school intake was increased to two classes and I was given one of these as my class.

Just before Easter 1949 we had a football match, boys v teachers. During the game I found difficulty in kicking the ball. My ankles were swelling up and I was running a temperature. The doctor came to see me then arranged for a consultant to visit. The result was that I was suffering from sub acute rheumatism, a mild form of rheumatic fever. It was two months before I was fit to return to school.

Two years later in 1951 there was a flu' epidemic which hit me badly. I was sent to hospital suffering from endocarditis. The rheumatism had affected a heart valve and an infection of this valve meant that it could not open and close properly.

Fortunately a new cure for this illness had recently been discovered. It involved six weeks of penicillin injections into my bottom every three hours night and day. Towards the end of the course I was asked by a nurse to help her restrain a patient who was behaving violently. I suffered a stroke as a result which paralysed one side of my body and affected my speech. After a few days I started to get better and was discharged from hospital but had to stay off school for four months in total. At the end of three months I was put on half pay. I returned to school but limited the extent of my exertions. I didn't go out at night, I walked rather than ran and sat down instead of standing.

It was during this period that Hilda was approached by a lady whose son was doing very badly in grammar school His overall position was 90th out of 90 at the end of the third year.

My friend Doug Tilley taught Maths at the grammar school. When I asked him about Michael, he said, "Don't touch him with a barge pole, he's hopeless".

As I was housebound in the evenings, I invited Michael to come round on a Wednesday evening when Hilda attended an evening class. I would ask him to do his Maths. homework. He was hopeless. He just guessed at answers. It became clear that he'd missed out in some elementary arithmetic in primary school, probably through absence due to illness. So I had to take him through elementary arithmetic. When he'd done it, I'd ask him, "Are you sure"? At first he was never sure but as he progressed he became more confident.

He came every Wednesday during his fourth year and until Easter in his fifth year. Not only was his confidence in Maths. improving but in all other subjects.

ALIAS CHARLIE

That Easter I moved from Doncaster to Beverley to become Head of Science at Longcroft School.

When the 'O' level results came Michael did well and at 'A' level he was showing promise. He went on to a pharmaceutical college where he was the outstanding student of the final year.

The year after my heart illness there was a boy in my technical class who had suffered badly with asthma in primary school. In my class he never had a day's absence. His mother told the Head that it was because of me. The way I'd overcome my illness and my relaxed attitude was such that her son had made a miracle cure.

Whether or not this was coincidental I am not sure but I do know that in many other respects I wasn't a great teacher. My classes were always the noisiest in the school. To make myself heard I used to have to shout. One day when I had a cold and could hardly speak I found the boys straining their ears to hear me and were exceptionally quiet. In future I resolved never to shout again.

One day when my class was working quietly away a little mouse popped his head through a hole in the wall and had a good look round. When it was spotted and someone shouted it darted back in again.

1951 the year of my long absence was the year I had been selected to go to Llandudno to the NUT Annual Conference. I was to be part of the Doncaster delegation going as the young teacher representative. I also missed out on a trip to London to see the Festival of Britain.

To compensate I was sent in 1952 to the Christmas Conference which was held in Church House, Westminster. This was a two day conference. I went again in 1953.

Doncaster NUT branch had put forward a motion that 'Secondary Modern Schools should be allowed to take external exams'. The motion was No. 3 on the programme. When No. 1 motion was called they weren't ready nor were the sponsors of motion No. 2. I found myself making the first speech at the conference. It wasn't something that I'd given much thought to. It had become evident that the 11+ exam failure meant that some pupils were not able to take exams which they were capable of passing when they were older.

I thought there would be opposition from the Birmingham delegates who had spoken quite strongly in the previous year. They were quick to assure the assembly that they were not opposed to the motion. The Deputy General Secretary of the NUT then got up and spoke at length in favour of the resolution which was carried.It was interesting to read in the following week's edition of the 'The Teacher', their report on the conference. I was given the credit for saying all the things the Deputy Genereal Secretary had said.

The 1944 Education Act had suggested that secondary modern schools should not be involved in external exams. This conference resolution was the first step towards the development of the CSE and later of the GCSE. Nowadays things have gone to the other extreme. Schools are being judged in league tables. This has put an unhelpful strain on pupils and teachers. I believe stress counselling for pupils and teachers is now common.

Chapter 31

After I'd been at Hyde Park School for six years, Hilda felt it was time I looked for promotion. I was perfectly happy at Hyde Park but one teacher, who was my junior, went off to become head of a primary school. I started to look in The Times Educational Supplement for possible posts.

I went to a technical school in Grimsby for a Head of Science post. The man who got the job travelled back in the train with me. He was a lecturer in an Emergency Training College which was about to close. These colleges were set up, after the war, to train people leaving the Forces who hadn't gone to training college or university but who'd shown ability whilst in the Forces.

He told me about some of the interviews he'd attended. On one occasion he was asked to meet the head at a London station. It started to rain so the interview was conducted in a 'phone box. Needless to say, the lecturer wasn't prepared to take any post without seeing the school first.

In my last year at Hyde Park I'd asked the head if I could take charge of the bottom class in the 4th year, the last year they would be in school. I still taught some Science but I had this class for Maths, English, History, Science and Games.

With the class came some of their exercise books from the previous year. When I looked at their work it seemed that every book contained discouraging phrases; 'Not good enough', 'See me', '3 out of 10'. It made sad reading. I thought, in their nine years of schooling they seemed to have learned very little. If they learn nothing from me I'd have done the same as their earlier teachers. If I can improve them that will be a feather in my cap. So instead of writing 'Poor effort 3/10', I started to write 'Quite a good try 6/10'. This soon became 'Good effort 7/10' and even 'Well done 8/10'

The effect was quite dramatic. Although the work was still of a very low standard they were starting to write quite long essays full of spelling mistakes. I well remember one boy, whom we called 'Plum' because of his ruddy complexion. One Monday morning he brought in an essay ten pages long. When I complimented him for doing so much work, he told me that on a Sunday morning they were required to stay in bed, so he spent his time writing this essay.

I felt my pupils with all their faults were beginning to try to do better.

I applied for the post of Head of Science at Longcroft School in Beverley. This school had only been opened about five years and I was the third person to be Head of Science. The first had gone after three years to be a head teacher elsewhere. His successor moved after two years to become senior mistress at another school.

Longcroft was built in what had been a large estate. The grounds were beautiful and spacious with many large trees. It backed on to Beverley racecourse and at afternoon break times you often saw the horses galloping along the racetrack. Longcroft was the first new school in the East Riding. It had been splendidly designed and was a showpiece.

In the Science department there was a teacher who specialised in Physics and another whose speciality was Biology. I found myself teaching General Science, a mixture of Physics, Chemistry and Biology.

The pupils came in at the age of 12+, a year later than in most secondary modern schools. They came from a large number of small villages. For some the daily journey to school took them into a completely new environment. I found their knowledge of the countryside and of the animals, birds and insects to be fascinating. On my first day a boy came into my lab., with a grass snake and asked if he could leave it in one of the sinks until he went home. He'd found it on his way to school and wanted to take it home as a pet. A pupil asked me if we could have a nature club at lunch time. I said I didn't know much about nature. He said they'd teach me. I remember going on to the playing field when it was covered with snow and being told what animals and birds had gone across from the foot prints in the snow.

One day a boy brought in the skin of a grass snake which he'd found in a loft. Normally when a snake sheds its skin as it gets larger it rolls the skin up and swallows it. This snake must have been disturbed before it was able to dispose of the skin. I remember a hedgehog curled up into a ball and then running to a hole at great speed. I'd no idea that hedgehogs could run so fast.

Pupils used to bring in the pellets vomitted up by owls. They would dissect these owl pellets which were full of little bones and fur and feathers from the birds and animals which the owl had eaten. When I wanted some caddis fly larvae, Robert Charlton, a friend of Robin, brought in about a hundred. The larva protects itself by sticking little stones or bits of wood to its outside when it spends its larval state at the bottom of a stream.

At the back of my lab. there was a nature table which was always full of interesting finds brought in by the pupils. I remember we got an injured bat and tried to keep it alive but it died on us as did injured birds we tried to feed. The pupils were learning from me and I was learning from the pupils.

We bought a detached house on the outskirts of Leconfield a village about four miles from Beverley. There was a very large garden. One part was an orchard with twenty apple trees, ranging from Bramleys to small dwarf trees. Each winter I would spray them with a tar oil and would be rewarded with masses of apples in the following autumn.

I decided to keep chickens in another part of the garden. I obtained a hen house and made a large chicken run where our six young hens thrived and provided us with eggs. Another part of the garden backed on to a blank wall of the house. Here I made a cricket wicket and used to bowl at Robin who was showing skill as a young cricketer. The garden was hard work but I enjoyed it.

By then Robin had left the infants' school and joined Susan who was in her last year at primary school. Hilda became pregnant again. We had four bicycles on which the four of us used to travel round the area. When Margaret was born we had to buy our first car, a pre-war Vauxhall 14 which was very roomy and had lovely leather seats. We were able to put Margaret in her cot on the back seat beside Hilda, Susan and Robin sat with me in the front.

I hadn't had a driving licence. Towards the end of my army time the officer in charge of transport had given us all a certificate saying we were qualified to drive a motor cycle and vehicles up to 3 tons in weight. I took this along to the licensing office where on the payment of 5 shillings I was given a driving licence. My family tend to remind me that the reason I'm not a good driver is because I never had to pass a test. Just the same it was me who took them out when they first learned to drive.

Leconfield was a friendly village to live in. At the Beverley side of the village was a large aerodrome. There were more people in the RAF houses than there were in the rest of the village. The flight path of the bombers used to take them over Longcroft School and when they went over you had to stop talking to your class until the sound died away.

Our house was open to the strong East wind and it could be very cold in winter but I found myself to be much healthier than I'd been in Doncaster.

Now that we had a car we were able to travel much further afield. We went to Bridlington, Hull, Hornsea and to Doncaster quite regularly and we got to know the East Riding very well.

Susan passed the 11+ exam and started to go to Beverley High School for Girls. Robin represented Beverley Junior Schools at football. Once Margaret was walking she used to carry the eggs from the hen house with great care. She never dropped one.

Longcroft School had started entering pupils for 'O' level exams with very satisfying results. In my 4th and final year there all my General Science pupils passed. The Director of Education, Victor Clarke, was keen that the secondary schools widespread through the East Riding should keep in regular contact with each other. The only subject teachers who met regularly were the science teachers. We visited various works and factories and held lecture sessions in schools and at Hull University. I really did learn a lot from our meetings. In time I became Secretary of the Science Teachers' Association.

Victor Clarke lived in the next village to Leconfield. Sometimes when he passed me at the bus stop he would stop and give me a lift. When he did, it was to ask my opinion on something or other. One morning he asked me what I thought about the pictures on the school walls. I had to confess that I hadn't really looked at them. When I got into school I made a point of looking at them. They were well worth seeing. When I did become a head teacher I always made a point of having good pictures in my room and throughout the school. We also made a point of having pupils' paintings on display.

A new secondary modern school was being built in Hornsea. The head master, Sidney Fox, was a classics master from a grammar school. I applied for the post of Deputy Head. As a Science teacher from a secondary modern school with a good track record, he felt that I would make a good deputy. I do think that we worked well together.

My appointment was to start at Easter 1958 but was delayed until my pupils had taken their 'O' levels.

The school did not open until September 1958 so that gave us good time to get things organised. The completion of the building was in some doubt because the builder had underestimated the cost of building it and had exceeded his credit level. In the end he could only get supplies by paying cash, However the school did open on time.

Chapter 32

We bought a very nice detached house near the Floral Hall in Hornsea, a few minutes walk away from the sea. Hornsea was a lovely, friendly small town and we soon began to make many new friends. The new school became the centre of many activities. Like Longcroft, it was built in what had been part of a large estate. It, too had trees that had been established many generations ago.

It was decided to set up a Caledonian Society in Hornsea, and I became President. Each month we used to meet in a small hall in the school where we danced to the music of Jimmy Shand played on gramophone records.

A well attended Evening Institute was formed where many people came to attend lessons and make friends. On a Friday evening there was a Youth Club which Susan attended. Susan unlike Rob was never really interested in sporting activities. However there was going to be a big Youth Club Dance to be held at Longcroft School. To qualify to go there you had to take part in the East Riding Youth Clubs Sports on the Saturday afternoon. Susan wanted to go to the dance but didn't know what activity she should enter at the Sports. Rob and I thought she should try putting the shot, so we three went down to the beach and had Susan putting large stones for practice. On the Friday night she went to the Youth Club and practised with a real shot. She achieved really long distances. However, on Saturday morning her arm was very swollen and painful but she was determined to go to the Sports. When she got there, there were only three girls who had entered for the shot. Susan picked it up and let it fall. She was given a certificate saying she'd come third. More to the point she was able to attend the dance in the evening.

Susan continued to attend Beverley High School. This meant

catching a bus at 8 a.m. Each morning Hilda would shout, "Lift up your hearts". This was the radio programme which came on at 7.50 a.m. and was the signal for Susan to go out to catch the bus. At the other end of Hornsea a lady would get on and join Susan upstairs. She would be eating some toast and when she'd finished she would start to put on her stockings.

Rob became a pupil in the first year. He was in a class of pupils, many of whom went on to achieve high academic success. He captained the first year football team and in the second year they won the East Riding cup. He also opened the batting for the school cricket team, playing in short trousers. At the end of the first season, caps were to be awarded to the best cricketers. Martin Lonsdale had put Rob's name forward together with some fourth year boys. Sidney Fox said, "We can't give a cap to a first former". Martin said, "He topped the batting averages, if he doesn't get a cap nobody else should". Rob got his cap. In his second year he was chosen to represent East Riding Schools, opening the batting and was awarded his East Riding cap.

He also joined Hornsea men's cricket club and became a regular in their 2nd team playing against men in the Hull and East Riding League.

In the summer the boys and girls from his class who lived in Hornsea used to go down to the beach straight after school. One Saturday afternoon I went down to the beach with him. He wanted to swim a quarter of a mile. There were two breakwaters which were 220 yards apart so the idea was that he would swim from one to the other then back. When he'd done that he kept going and in the end he swam a mile. It took him more that an hour to do it.

When Margaret was four and a half she started going to the reception class at the primary school. Hilda took her each day and in this way got to know the other mothers. Amongst these was Margaret Strangward. Margaret had been a nurse before she married Geoff who had a chemist's shop and also worked as an optician upstairs. Our two families became very friendly and when we left Hornsea to go to Sussex they used to come and stay with us and likewise we used to go to stay with them in Hornsea. We have kept in touch ever since.

Susan and her friends used to meet in the Floral Hall on a Sunday afternoon to have a long chat over a cup of something to drink or an ice cream. In the evening they went to the Primitive Methodist Church where they sat in the balcony joining in the singing.

I found myself embroiled in the PTA and also in the other Methodist church's mens' study group. John Hall who had been a colleague at Longcroft was now head of a primary school in the next village. He lived in the next street to us. He invited me to go with him. Once I'd attended I was roped in. The discussions were often lively. One man who was retired but had been an HMI (school inspector) would listen to the discussion then take part near the end with some well chosen words.

All our married life, Hilda attended evening classes. In Hornsea she went to cookery classes. She was already an excellent cook but was always keen to try something different. She was also very good at sewing and made clothes for all the family. She was a full time mother and we all benefitted.

When the school had been open about a year. Victor Clarke called in. Sydney Fox was not immediately available and I started to show him around. He said he was particularly impressed at the way the school had developed so quickly. It was true. We had an excellent staff who worked well together. I keep in touch with many of them. On my 70th birthday my family arranged a surprise birthday party for me at Margaret's house, near Thirsk. I was delighted to see so many of my old friends from Hornsea who'd come to join the party.

Chapter 33

Sydney Fox had been teaching in a grammar school in Wales. There they had a kind of Eisteddfod each year. He decided we should have an Arts Festival each year. On periods 7 and 8 on a Thursday the school would divide into house groups. Each pupil was expected to take part in at least one activity. They had to be in a play, or choir or choral verse group. Just before Easter a whole day would be taken up by the Arts Festival where each house put on its performances in the school hall. Round the school were displayed articles and paintings produced by individual pupils. Competition was very keen and the house spirit developed strongly. In the summer term the activities were different. Many pupils were involved in various sports. I started a naturalist's society which many of the first year boys joined.

At one side of Hornsea there is a large freshwater lake called Hornsea Mere. It was less than a mile from the school and about the same distance from the sea. In between the land was mainly meadow.

In the Mere there were a number of small islands where swans nested. There was quite a large variety of freshwater fish and insects. Over the meadow there was a profusion of birds. There were sea birds, fresh water birds and meadow and woodland birds all to be seen at the same time.

I took my group down to the Mere. Here we saw a range of wild flowers rarely seen elsewhere. We would try to identify as many as we could. Near the sea there were lots of fossils, ammonites and belemnites being the most common. One day the lads found some stones with sharp edges. They were sure they were tools that had been used by some form of early civilisation based on the Mere. They imagined people living in huts on stilts by the lake. Imagination ran wild. They kept finding new tools.

Robert Stirling

When it was time to pack up they asked to stay longer. After an extra hour I said we had to finish. They wanted to know if they could come with me on Saturday morning. I said, "No. I'll be busy on Saturday. We'll carry on next Thursday".

The following week one of the boys said he'd been thinking about our finds. His view was that, that part of the lake had been dredged and this would account for so many stones being cracked and forming sharp edges. We thought about it and agreed that this was the most likely explanation.

We made some nets out of an old lace curtain and used them to fish in the Mere. We collected different types of plankton and insect larvae which we would try to identify. Some of these we would take back to a glass tank in the lab and spend time looking at them through microscopes and hand lenses.

One parent spent the best part of a Sunday trying to separate a huge ammonite from the rock in which it was set. When he'd almost got it out, it came to pieces for which he was severely castigated by his son.

Another parent was the mate on a sea going trawler which sailed from Hull on long trips to the fishing grounds near Iceland. With the fish they caught in the nets were many sea creatures which I did not know existed. I used to give him some formalin and he would dilute this with sea water and bring the creatures back in empty pickle jars. I forget all the things he brought back but I do remember creatures he called sea mice and sea spiders. One trip he came back with six baby octopuses. Apparently they were born in the sea off the coast of the West Indies. They were carried all the way to Iceland by the Gulf Stream. Cod devour them and when there is a good catch of cod there are also many octopuses scrambling round the deck and are thrown back into the sea.

We had a rural science teacher who looked after the greenhouse and a school garden. As was my wont since my days at Hyde Park I enjoyed taking bottom ability groups for Science. One day I was taking this class to look at things in the garden. There was this timid little girl who had no father at home. She took my hand in hers. I was tempted to withdraw particularly as we could be seen from within the school but I decided to let her hold my hand if this gave her a sense of security. It was Autumn and many of the flowers and weeds had gone to seed. We collected some, noting how they were dispersed naturally. We planted some of the seeds in seed boxes which we kept in the lab. The only seeds that grew for us were French marigolds. Many plants require a frost before the seeds will grow.

As was the case at Longcroft I was continually learning new things about nature.

In my third year at Hornsea I thought I would start applying for a headship. Sidney Fox had suggested to the LEA that I should be paid extra because I was doing two jobs. Deputy Head and Head of Science. The authority didn't agree. I started to look in the Times Educational Supplement. I applied for two schools in the North Riding, one at Northallerton and the other at Saltburn. In each case it was a foregone conclusion that the local school governors would choose someone they knew.

I applied for a school in Petworth in Sussex and was called for a preliminary interview in Chichester which was conducted by the Deputy Director of Education and the lady advisor. I returned to Hornsea feeling that I'd blown my chance. A few days later I was called to come to Petworth in West Sussex to be interviewed for the post of Headmaster of the Herbert Shiner Secondary Modern School. Since the school was in the process of being built the interview was to be held in the local Trust House Hotel.

I travelled from Hornsea to Petworth on the day before the interview and booked in at the hotel. I went to look at the school and made enquiries about houses for sale in Petworth. I was told there were none. Only three houses had been built since the war. One was for Lord Leconfield's niece, another for a lady who was a councillor and a third in the grounds of the rectory.

When I learned that the village and all the land surrounding it belonged to the Leconfield family, it struck me that fate was going to direct me back to my connection with Leconfield in the East Riding.

In the morning there were five of us to be interviewed. It was done in alphabetical order. I was No. 4 on the list. The first three were interviewed in the morning. We then adjourned for lunch. I sat at the same table as Lady Shakerley. She asked me in which part of Hornsea did I live. I told her I lived near the Floral Hall. She said her old nanny lived near there and that she often went up to Hornsea to see her.

After lunch I went in for interview. I sensed that I was the preferred candidate. Because of the housing situation I had decided I didn't want the job. The less keen I became the more anxious they were to have me. After the last candidate had been interviewed I was summoned to go back in to be offered the post. I explained that I couldn't really accept because of the housing situation. They said they would build me a new house but in the meantime we would be accommodated in Culvercroft the dower house next to Petworth House. I accepted the post on that understanding.

Chapter 34

Petworth, situated in West Sussex, is a small rural town on the main road from London to Chichester, four miles north of the South Downs. The Herbert Shiner School which was in the process of being built was named after Sir Herbert Shiner, the Chairman of West Sussex County Council. He was a remarkable man, a police constable in London before the First World War, he rose from the ranks in the army to become a major. At the end of the war he, with the Rev Tubby Clayton started the charitable institution Toc H. Toc stood for T in the code then used and Toc H was the intials for Talbot House in France.

When we arrived in Petworth it was in many respects medieval. It had not altered much during the last 300 years.

The whole area belonged to the Leconfield family. The third Baron Leconfield died in 1952 aged 80. In 1947 he gave Petworth House with 735 acres of park land to the National Trust. At his death he was one of the greatest land owners in Britain, owning about 150,000 acres in Sussex and Cumberland. He was very fond of hunting but as he got older he could no longer jump the fences. He had a servant who opened the gates for him. The servant was known locally as John the Baptist, because he preceded the Lord.

Lord Leconfield left his famous collections of paintings to his nephew, Mr John Wyndham who lived in part of Petworth House with his family. John Wyndham was private secretary to Harold MacMillan who was then prime minister. When Harold MacMillan retired and became Baron Stockton, John Wyndham was given the title Lord Egremont, which had been the family title in earlier times.

The school governors were a fairly powerful lot. Sir Herbert Shiner was Chairman. John Wyndham, Lady Shakerley, Mrs

Evershed the wife of Admiral Evershed were some of the influential people. Sir Herbert Shiner told me, "If you find you are having problems, give me a ring before 8 a.m. and I'll look into the matter". I never did ring him. I didn't want to cause any trouble at the Education Office.

Whilst I was still in Hornsea, I had to think about staff appointments. The first post to be filled was that of Deputy Head. When it was advertised in the Times Educational Supplement there were 250 applicants. Each day there would be large pile of applications forwarded to my home by the Education Office. Each night I would go through them and give them a mark out of ten. In the end the shortlist was made of people who had got 9/10 or 9½ out of ten. Ivor Astley who got the post at the interview had got the mark 9½ out of ten. He was then Head of History at a London Comprehensive School.

The school was due to open in September 1951 with a first year intake of 80 pupils and a small staff. I started in May and had the reponsibility of ordering all the furniture and equipment we would need. I was given a sum of money and being a careful Scot I spent it cannily. In Hornsea School we had some furniture made by Remploy and as far as practicable I ordered from them. Remploy was an organisation funded by the government which provided employment for disabled people and particularly victims of war injury.

As a family we moved into Culvercroft, a large mansion which had been built for a Dowager Lady Leconfield. At the time of our moving in, the ground floor was occupied by the boys' primary school. We had the use of the top floor. After the primary school moved out to their newly built primary school building we had the mansion to ourselves. Hilda decided to paper one room as a play room for Margaret. It took 26 rolls of wallpaper.

The house that had been promised was built in the middle of a new council estate but there was no way Hilda was going to live in a council estate. The house was altered to accommodate one married teacher and family and to provide two detached flats for two single teachers.

Some land was bought beside the school and a new headmaster's house was built there. Lady Egremont once asked Hilda why we didn't want to continue living in Culvercroft. Hilda replied, "We can't afford to keep it heated". In the various rooms there were large stoves which required a lot of coal to keep them burning.

In the summer it was a lovely house. There was a large walled garden and an all weather tennis court. The education authority still paid for a gardener to look after things but that would have ceased if we were going to live there permanently. To maintain the house would require an army of servants. We lived there for two years before our new house was ready for occupation.

Susan and Rob travelled each day to Midhurst Grammar School, Susan in the 6th form, Rob in the 3rd year. Margaret attended Petworth Girls' Primary School. She was too much in advance of the other girls of her age so she was moved to another building where the girls were two and three years older than her. She wasn't happy in that class so we decided to take her to a convent school in Midhurst where one of our friends sent her children. Here she enjoyed herself and proved to be quite clever.

The social structure in Petworth was interesting. There were the gentry and there were the people who worked for them. In between there was a small group, the vets, doctors, bank manager and some others. Hilda was invited to join the Luncheon Club. Many of the members were meeting for coffee at one of their members house and Hilda was asked to come there first. She had expected them to be drinking coffee but most of them were having gin. Many of the wives had so little to do that they were alcoholics. There was a group of ladies who provided refreshments for old folk in a small hall. Hilda was on duty one day when Lady Shakerly asked her to help the other lady because she had just come out of an alcoholics clinic.

Petworth Primary School was housed in three separate buildings. On Michaelmass Day 1942 a German bomber was being chased by a British fighter plane. The Germans jettisoned their bombs. One landed directly on the boys' school killing the 2 teachers and 27 boys. There was this gap in the age group of men who'd been raised in Petworth.

Robert Stirling

One of my first duties on arrival at Petworth was to open the Summer Fair. The Fair was to have been opened by a film actor, John Bentley, who lived in Petworth. His film work took him away at that time and so the committee decided to ask the new headmaster to do the honours. I crowned the Carnival Queen and made a little speech then went round buying from the various stalls.

On another occasion the BBC decided to broadcast the Friday night radio show 'Any Questions', from the Herbert Shiner School. Hilda and I went as part of the invited audience. I forget the name of the chairman but two of the panel members were Isobel Barnett and Professor Asa Briggs.

Sir Herbert Shiner died rather suddenly and the new Chairman of Governors, George Mant, and I went to his private funeral in a little village church. Among the mourners was the Duke of Norfolk, a leading Catholic. George Mant said that Sir Herbert must have been very highly regarded for the Earl Marshal to have attended. Later there was a memorial service in Chichester Cathedral where all the leading institutions of the county were represented. It made me realise the power of the Establishment.

About a year after the school was open a governors' meeting took place. On the agenda was what arrangements were to be made for the official opening of the school. John Wyndham said he would invite Sir Edward Boyle, the Minister for Education, to come and stay with him some weekend and the opening of the school could be done then.

It was arranged for the ceremony to take place on a Saturday afternoon. Before the opening there was a lunch in the school which Hilda and I attended. During the lunch I mentioned to Edward Boyle that he had opened Hornsea School when I was Deputy Head. He said he remembered me. When he spoke to the audience he told them I was an old friend of his. The blessing was given by the Rev Tubby Clayton. After the ceremony Tubby asked me if it would be alright to phone some of his friends whilst he was down in Sussex. I showed him to my office. The next hour he spent on the phone, I could hear him saying, "Hello . . . this is Tubby".

ALIAS CHARLIE

When I was interviewed for the headship, the Director of Education knew that I'd been Secretary of the East Riding Science Teachers' Association. He was keen that a West Sussex Association be formed. One Saturday all the secondary school headteachers were invited to the Herbert Shiner School for the day. Amongst the other business the Director wanted me to explain the need for such an association particularly as the prospect of the CSE exams was being promoted nationally. We had lunch and Dr. Read wanted me to sit at lunch with him and some HMIs but I chose to sit with some other heads. The result of the meeting was that a Science Teachers' Association would be formed and I was given the task of organising it.

One of our first visits was to a very large nursery on the South coast. There they grew chrysanthemums and carnations in very large greenhouses. Flowers were sent to Covent Garden Market on 52 weeks of the year so they had this system of making the conditions inside the greenhouses the same for each day of the year. In the summer the shades were drawn to give 12 hours of darkness. In winter heating and lighting were used to replicate the same conditions. It was essential that no plants grew too soon or too slowly. We were told that at one time they also grew tomatoes but they couldn't compete with nurseries in Surrey which were on a South facing slope and received more sunlight as a consequence.

The CSE exams and syllabuses had to be devised. We divided the science panel into 4 groups, General Science, Physics, Chemistry and Biology. Each panel would meet separately and would send a representative to the Southern Examining Board which was being set up. I acted as coordinator sending out to schools the details of the work being done by the various panels.

Chapter 35

Once when we were on holiday in Sutton Sea we met Rupert Moore who was walking along the sea front. Rupert had been captain in charge of Welfare in the same Highland Brigade where I was Education Officer. We had been good friends then so it was nice to meet him again. At the time he was living in Skegness but when I went to Petworth he was living in Chichester. Our two families became very friendly.

Another old friend was Alex Crawford. We had lived in the same street in Clydebank and were in the same group that went about together. He kept in contact with us during the war. Alex rose to become a major. I stayed with him and his wife when I went to the NUT conference in London. He was now living in Eastbourne and we had the chance to meet again.

Whilst at the Herbert Shiner School I went to many meetings of the secondary head teachers. I also went on a number of courses. I remember one was about teaching French to primary school pupils. Another was on Evening Institutes or Night Schools. It was emphasised that the scope of these institutes should be widened to include recreational activities in addition to vocational training. I decided to open a Centre for Leisure Activities to take place at the school in the evenings. At first there was difficulty about using this name because the Education Committee had to agree to pay. Agreement was given and we opened with courses on gardening, cooking, dressmaking, woodwork and badminton. I asked Hilda to take the dressmaking class which became very popular and always ran on past closing time.

One of my contributory primary schools urgently needed a temporary teacher. Hilda was approached and although not a teacher she helped them out for a few weeks. She had to ask Margaret what she should do with her class. I soon got fed up with Hilda setting off in the morning before me and as soon as a replacement was found we were able to get back to normal.

At Midhurst Grammar School, Rob soon got into the school cricket team then in winter into the school rugby team. In the following year he was playing rugby and cricket for West Sussex schools then he became a regular for Sussex Schoolboys' Cricket team. He won an award which allowed him to go, one Easter, to Sussex Club's ground at Hove to be coached by professionals. He was also selected to go to Lilleshal Sports Centre where they were coaching boys for the England Schoolboys Cricket Team.

Rob also played for Petworth Park Cricket Team which played to a high standard in a Sussex league. Home matches were played in the grounds of Petworth Park. The only snag about this was that it was a deer park and when you were fielding in the outfield you had to be careful not to tread in deer pats.

Midhurst School played their home games in Cowdray Park which was part of the estate of Lord Cowdray. Next to the cricket field was the polo pitch. A regular polo player was Prince Philip and the Queen often presented the trophy to the winning team.

I was made a Vice President of Petworth Cricket Club along with many others. It was their way of getting a few more subscriptions. Another Vice President was Fred Streeter who used to do the gardening programme on TV. He was the head gardener at Petworth Park and lived on the other side of the high wall from Culvercroft. Annually he presented a cricket bat to the most promising player. One year Rob was the recipient.

I was also coopted on to the committee of the Church of England Children's Society. Lady Egremont was President. Among the others on the committee were Mrs Beaufoy and Mrs de Pass. Mrs de Pass lived in a large house next to the Herbert Shiner School. Every Wednesday morning a helicopter would land on her field to take her to London where she had her hair done and did some shopping.

Mrs Beaufoy was a very kind wealthy widow. She provided financial support to many activities. Some people, down on their luck were able to buy their groceries from the main grocer. Mrs Beaufoy would pay their bills each week.

There were other ladies who were well off in the committee. It was decided we would have a sale of second hand clothes and other articles at Petworth House. Two men who were on the paid staff of the Society helped to organise it.

All the ladies had clothes they wanted to donate so that they had an excuse to buy more. The problem was that they did not know how to set about selling the clothes. I said I'd ask Hilda to see to it. Hilda came with a measuring tape and arranged the clothes on hangers according to size. She put a price on each article.

On the Friday night everything was ready. The London wine merchants who supplied wine and spirits to Lord Egremont had donated a lot of wine and spirits. After a few drinks the evening was a great success and produced a hefty profit for charity.

In the scrap book, which Hilda kept throughout the war and later, is a note from Lady Egremont's secretary asking Hilda to come round to tell them how to dispose of the unsold clothes.

Some time later a new theatre was opened in Chichester. It was called Theatre in the Round. The stage came out into the middle of the theatre and the audience sat around. On the opening night Princess Margaret was to attend. Lord and Lady Egremont had booked seats in the circle close to where the Princess would sit. At the last moment they were unable to go and they asked Hilda and I to go in their place. So we found ourselves sitting amongst the nobility watching George Bernard Shaw's St. Joan starring Joan Plowright and Norman Rossington.

Ivor Astley, my deputy, was on the CSE History Panel. We used to discuss ways of broadening historical interest. It was then I started to write my book, "The story of the atom". One lunchtime I thought, a "History of Medicine" might be a good option. I jotted down a few names, Semmelweiss, Lister, Harvey, Pasteur, Jenner and some others and gave it to Ivor. The next time he went to the CSE panel meeting they decided to include this as an option and the syllabus based on my names was used for many years by the Southern CSE Examination Board.

In our third year at the Herbert Shiner School we both were considering moving on. Ivor applied for a headship in Derbyshire which he got.

ALIAS CHARLIE

There was a school in Ipswich for which I was shortlisted. Hilda and I decided we'd go and look at it. We set off one Sunday on a sunny February morning and arrived at the school just before lunch. From the outside it looked to be a good school in a good area and I thought it would be worth going for the interview. We had barely set off on the return journey when a stone hit the windscreen and the whole screen shattered. It was impossible to see where we were going so I had to take most of the screen out. The journey back was horrendous. The weather was very cold and the air coming in onto our faces and round our necks was bitterly cold and we had to drive slowly for the next three hours. When we got back to Culvercroft I decided that this was an omen so I wrote to say I wouldn't be attending the interview.

After Susan passed her 'A' levels she went to Goldsmiths College in London to train to become a teacher. She was sent to an address where accommodation had been arranged for her. I took her there with her luggage only to find that Susan's name wasn't on the list the landlady had been given. I rang the College and they suggested we go to an address a few doors away. This lady didn't know that she was getting a student until we arrived. She gave Susan accommodation in a conservatory which wasn't at all satisfactory. Susan stayed there till Christmas until she was able to find something better.

At Goldsmiths Susan joined the choir and took part in Handel's Messiah. Hilda and I went up to see the performance which was really good. On the way back we were travelling along the main road when without any warning we hit a blanket of fog. I braked and veered to the left of the vehicle in front. Cars and lorries were coming in at speed behind us and we were lucky not to be involved in a collision. We crawled through the fog until the way was clear again. It was a most unnerving experience.

Chapter 36

I applied for the post of headteacher at a new school. Nunthorpe Secondary Modern in North Yorkshire and was invited to come for interview in Northallerton. Since the interview was not at the school I assumed that it was going to be a preliminary interview. We travelled by car stopping to drop off Margaret with Hilda's eldest sister, Eva, in Doncaster.

When we arrived at County Hall I told Hilda that I'd be in for about an hour. When I went in I found it was not a preliminary interview. A governing body had not yet been appointed for the new school so the candidates were being interviewed by the Secondary Education Committee.

When I went in, Colonel Jackson, who was the Chairman, looked through my written application and remarked, "I see you've found the best road in Scotland, the road to England". I replied, "I came down as a missionary". He roared with laughter. The others gave me a look which suggested, "What have we got here"?

However the interview went smoothly and at the end I was called in to be offered the job which I was happy to accept.

Nunthorpe is a village on the edge of Middlesbrough and the new school was still being built.

Meanwhile, in Petworth, there was to be a Governors' meeting on the following day. The main item on the agenda was a proposal that Midhurst Grammar School would become a Comprehensive School and that Midhurst Modern School and Sir Herbert Shiner School should become intermediate schools taking in pupils for two years only.

Major Mant was very much against the proposal. I rang him in the morning to tell him I was going back to Yorkshire. I also rang Dr. Read. At the meeting I spoke in favour of the scheme and it was accepted.

ALIAS CHARLIE

Hilda and I had not been entirley happy about staying on in Petworth. There didn't seem to be a future for us there. The money we had, from the sale of our house in Hornsea, was losing value as the price of houses kept increasing. Hilda, in particular, was glad to be going back to Yorkshire where most of our real friends were.

Unlike the East Riding and West Sussex authorities I wasn't employed by the North Riding until the September when the school was due to open. I came up to Nunthorpe to interview staff but most of the work I'd done in Petworth was done by the LEA. The main appointments were for Deputy Head and Senior Mistress. Six candidates had been chosen for me. Three men and three women. The selection of the Senior Mistress was no problem. Frances Allen was the obvious choice. Of the men, Col. Jackson preferred one from the Guisborough School where he was Chairman of Governors. I preferred John Howard, a history teacher from another school. It became a battle of wills and in the end Col. Jackson gave way. The Education Officer who was the third person on the panel expressed no opinion. He told me later that this was the first time he'd seen Col. Jackson give way. John turned out to be an excellent appointment and three years later he was appointed to the headship of a school in Scarborough.

During the Whitsun Holiday, Hilda and I came up to North Yorkshire to look for a home. Again we left Margaret with Eva in Doncaster. We didn't want to live too close to the school this time. In Petworth parents would think nothing of coming to our house on a Sunday morning with some query or other. This time I wanted to keep school and home apart from each other. We were very fortunate in finding the house we wanted in Redcar. It was a four bedroomed detached house overlooking a little park with a clear view to the sea. This was in 1964 and I am still living there in the year 2000.

When I interviewed for a school secretary it was the first meeting of the school governors. Again I was very lucky to find an outstanding secretary in Peggy Smith. During the war Peggy had been in the ATS and we ran the office much as things were done in the Army.

Throughout the Summer holiday, Peggy, John and I sorted out all the equipment arriving for the new school. We had a gem of a school caretaker, Joe Cook, who had been a miner in West Yorkshire. He held the world record for Tip Cat. This was a game where a piece of wood was balanced on a stone. You hit the wood at the end with your club and as it flies up you give it a great whack. I remember the P.E. advisor for the North Riding coming to see Joe giving a demonstration.

I held a parents' meeting before the school opened to explain to them how I wanted to see the school develop. In particular I said we would be entering pupils for GCE exams as well as CSE.

Many years later a parent accosted me in Stokesley. He said, "When you said that pupils would be doing GCE, at that first meeting, I didn't believe you". No other secondary modern school in the North Riding was doing so. This parent had twins. The girl had passed the 11+ exam but the boy hadn't. In the event they both got the same number of 'O' levels. The boy did better at 'A' level and went on to become a dentist. In those days failing the 11+ exam could be a family disaster.

The school opened with a first year intake of a hundred pupils and another 200 second, third and fourth year pupils in total. The parents of these children were given the option of sending their children to Nunthorpe or leaving them at their existing school. The original first year pupils produced some very clever people who went on to University.

Hilda attended an evening class on tailoring for two years and made clothes for the grandchildren and the rest of the family. When the tailor left she decided to go to an evening course on golf. The result of this was that we both joined Cleveland Golf Club. During term time Hilda used to play on a Tuesday and I played on a Sunday morning. It was great to get rid of the angst which built up during the week by smacking a golf ball round eighteen holes.

As we did at Hornsea and Petworth we had an interhouse Arts Festival each year. I chose the names of the four houses, Keller, Nightingale, Pasteur and Shaftesbury. They were four people whom I felt had done something worthwhile with their lives.

138

ALIAS CHARLIE

Captain Cook was born in our catchment area and the school badge took note of this. It had a Yorkshire Rose, a symbol for Cleveland Bay and a globe representing Cook's journeys.

The school motto, "To thine own self be true", was taken from the speech by Polonious to Laertes giving him advice as he was proposing to leave Denmark. "This above all, to thine own self be true, and it must follow as the night, the day, thou can'st not then be false to any man".

As a secondary modern school we were able to take part in many activities. There was always a Christmas tea and concert for the old folk. Each class produced a parcel and we would take them out to the old folk on the last day of term. The last two periods on a Wednesday were given to activities. Some pupils went to the homes of the elderly to help do gardening or run errands. But the thing the older people wanted was just to talk to the young people. Often they were housebound and rarely had visitors. Our young pupils would come after school and do things for them even if it was just talking over a cup of tea. It gave the pupils a realisation of the problems of the elderly. In morning assembly I would tell pupils that rowdy behaviour was very frightening to old people. I used to tell them about the newspaper boy in our street in Doncaster. He was always so cheerful as he went on his rounds. One old man looked forward each morning to his arrival. When the old man died he left a hundred pounds, in his will, to the newspaper boy. In 1950 that was a lot of money.

As an exercise for some boys in woodwork, I got them to build a chicken house and chicken run. Then I bought six hens and Percy a cock. They became the focus of interest for many pupils. I gave the keys to two twin boys who'd been in trouble in their previous school. They had the responsibility of looking after the hens. On school days the eggs collected belonged to the school, at weekends and holidays they belonged to the twins. Never were hens so well looked after. The twins and their friends came early in the morning, turned up without fail at the weekends and holidays, kept the henhouse tidy and became model pupils.

Wherever possible we tried to give pupils responsibility. One lad who had part of his stomach removed was given the job switching off unnecessary lights in the school hall and corridors. This little job gave him authority and cut down the electricity bill considerably.

We had a school gardener who was meticulous in care of the grounds. He and Joe Cook worked well together. At the front of the school there was this large lawn. Now that I had this golfing bug I asked them to make a putting course out of it. We bought the markers for the 18 holes. It was amazing how popular it became. Pupils made putters in woodwork or metalwork and before school and at lunch times the green was packed with players. I arranged for the local golf professional to come and give lessons to some pupils. We had some lads who became good golfers and as a school our team of three golfers were runners up in the English Schools Championships, one year. This was later on when the school became comprehensive. One of the trio went on to win the British Amateur Golf Championship which allowed him to play in the Open Championships, in Britain and in America and also in the American Masters. Sadly when the school became comprehensive we lost the putting green. It became a car park. We also lost our chickens and hen run.

I had always favoured the idea of the comprehensive school. Clydebank High School was comprehensive in its intake. The idea that a child's future could be decided at the age of eleven by a few tests seemed wrong. Nunthorpe School was in a favoured area and was able to provide enough clever pupils to allow for pupils taking 'O' levels in many subjects. Other schools in less favoured areas found it more difficult to provide the range of subjects to 'O' level standard. I've often wondered whether some of these children would have fared better by being selected for a grammar school. Also to cater for all abilities a comprehensive school needs to be large. In the large school the relations between teachers, and between teachers and pupils tend to become more impersonal.

With the advent of computers and the internet it might be worth considering having smaller comprehensive schools.

Chapter 37

In 1973 the school became comprehensive. It was being expanded from a school of five hunded pupils to one of a thousand pupils. This meant that a lot of new building had to be done. All round the school extensions were being carried out. I was greatly concerned that exits were being blocked and that pupils might be trapped if there was a fire. I contacted the fire service and they sent an officer to inspect the school. His verdict was that there were plenty of windows through which people could escape.

We had our first intake of 200 pupils. Shortly afterwards we were notified that using the school hall might be dangerous. The concrete beams supporting the roof were made of high alumina cement. This was a method used to make concrete beams where the concrete would harden quickly. Across the country there were examples occuring of pieces of concrete breaking off. All architects were contacted to check whether or not they'd used these beams.

The result was that we were unable to use the hall and stage for school use. We kept getting new furniture for classrooms which hadn't been completed so we used the stage as a store. There was no prospect of the repair work being done in the near future. I said to the school advisor, "The only way we'll get something done is to set fire to the place". This was said in jest but two weeks later it happened.

One Friday afternoon at 2 p.m. I heard Harry Tovey, the Head of Upper School, shout to the secretaries that the stage was alight and for them to set off the fire alarm. When the bell started to ring it was thought at first that it was ringing for the change of lessons at 2 p.m.

I dashed out of my office and saw Harry run to the stage with the idea of trying to put out the fire. By now the stage curtains were ablaze and I shouted to Harry, "Leave it". He then dashed up the stairs to direct people away from that staircase. I stood at the door ready to let anyone out who came my way. Two of the three secretaries were in the office, one kept her finger on the bell while the other phoned the fire brigade.

The plastic chairs on the stage started to give off a thick black smoke and within seconds it was travelling throughout the main building of the school. I slipped out through a door into the corridor when I could no longer see anything. The two secretaries weren't able to get out of their usual door into the foyer which was covered in the thick black smoke. There was another door leading into a quadrangle but they couldn't find the key. Peggy got a heavy typist's chair and smashed the glass so that they could scramble out. There was no way out of the enclosed quadrangle so they had to smash another window to get into the staff room which was filling up with smoke. They were unable to open a window. The window frames had recently been painted and they were stuck by the paint. They were seen by a workman who smashed another window to get them out onto the playing field. Peggy had a number of cuts on her arms and had to go to hospital to get them dressed. She also damaged an ankle jumping out of a window.

Meanwhile the pupils were being lined up in their positions in the playground which we had often practised during fire drills. Teachers checked that all their pupils were there. I sent Eddie Harland, the teacher in charge of the Lower School, to the primary school next door to check that the fire brigade was coming and to notify the Education Officer.

When the fire engines arrived we didn't know where to connect the hoses. The firepoints should have been marked by the letters FP on the walls. This had not been done. The architect in charge of the original building had assumed that it would be done by the Fire Brigade. The Fire Brigade said it should have been done by the architect. Eventually some points were found, one under a large puddle, and the fire hoses were attached.

We learned a lot from this disaster. The doors at the back of the stage which led to the changing rooms of the gymnasium should have been fire doors but they weren't. They soon burned down and if any girls had been upstairs in the girls' changing room they wouldn't have been able to get out.

The stage curtains should not have caught fire so easily. They should have been fireproofed.

What caused the fire we never found out. It might have been an electrical fault.

Every wall and ceiling was covered with a thick black layer and the smell was horrible.

On Saturday morning Hilda and I went in to see the devastation. The Deputy Chief Education Officer came in. We decided only the upper school pupils should come in on the Monday. Fortunately the upper school building wasn't affected nor were the science labs. and practical rooms.

In 1967 the school had been transferred from the North Riding Education Authority to a newly formed council, Teesside which was mainly Middlesbrough. The Chief Education Officer and his deputy lived in Nunthorpe close to the school so they were well aware of what was happening in the school.

Teachers were required to go to Middlesbrough General Hospital for a check up to make sure they were clear of infections. When I went I was X-rayed. The X-ray showed that I had an enlarged heart. An appointment was made for me to see a consultant. The first thing he said to me was, "How are you managing, after the fire"? He told me his daughter was one of the new first year pupils.

A team of workmen came into school to scrub down the walls, ceilings and furniture. It was a very big job and took quite a while. The rooms had then to be decorated and rewired. Pupils in the first two years were attending school for half days only.

When I think of all the problems we had over the years I am grateful that we didn't have any pupils seriously injured.

Before the school opened it was struck by lightning a number of times before the lightning conductors were fitted. There was one classroom on the fourth floor with a good all round view of the area, the industrial works of Middlesbrough to the North and the Cleveland hills and countryside to the South. This was the geography room. Also on the same level was a very large tank where all the water was stored. This water fed the various taps and toilets and also the boiler warming the school's heating system. Circulation of hot water depended on the head of water in this tank. After the fire the pumping system was improved by altering the direction of the flow.

When we first opened in 1964 workmen were still finishing things off. There was a glass door between the main building and a quadrangle which shattered. The clerk of Works on the site blamed the pupils for the damage. One day shortly after it had been repaired he went to go through the door when it suddenly flew open and shattered. The shape of the quadrangle was such that the wind hitting the high wall of the main building was reflected back in such a way that a vacuum was formed causing the door to fly open. Screens had to be built to stop this happening again.

The central heating system wasn't entirely satisfactory. The thermostats in the classrooms were situated next to the grilles where the hot air came out. They only measured the temperature of this air but not the temperature within the room. When I complained to the Senior Architect of the North Riding, he said, "If you had the money you'd buy a Rolls Royce but if you haven't you'll settle for a cheap car". That was the problem, money. In fact when they started to build the school they found it was over a layer of peat. This meant that they had to spend more money on the foundations than they'd expected.

Under the school was a duct through which gas pipes and electric cables ran. Also excess drain water ran through. Once during a period of exceptional rain the water flowing through this duct flooded the boiler room and put all controls out of action. The school had to close for three days whilst repairs were done.

When the gas supply changed from coal gas to natural gas from the North Sea, we kept getting gas leaks. Every cooking oven in the kitchen had leaks. Many of the pipes in the labs started to leak. The whole system of metal pipes had to be replaced by plastic tubing which was buried underground on the outside of

1st March 1943

the school. No electric cables or gas pipes now went through the underground duct.

When it came to the question of how to repair the school hall there was the problem of removing the long heavy concrete beams. The roof had been destroyed so the beams were exposed. A workman thought he'd hit one beam with a sledge hammer. It started to crumble and after a few more blows it fell to the ground. I used to keep some samples of that concrete which I could break off by hand. It really was a danger.

A new roof was put on fitted to plywood beams. There was no need for a heavy roof. There was nothing on top of it.

During the building of the extensions the workmen caused two fires. One was in one of their huts which they managed to put out with their own extinguisher. Another was on a roof being tarred when they needed to borrow an extinguisher from the school.

A workman was laying plastic tiles in the school foyer. He went off, probably to go to the toilet, leaving his blow torch burning. I turned it off.

There were many other problems. Cracks appeared on parts of a concrete wall on one staircase. I reported this and glass slides were stuck over the cracks. The thought was that if there was movement of the building the glass would crack. It never did.

When all the building had been completed the school bell system didn't function in some rooms. The officer of the LEA who had responsibility for repairs blamed the pupils and had all the bells raised out of their reach. I had to do a series of exercises where classes stayed in their rooms when they didn't hear the fire bell. Eventually he agreed that a new more powerful system had to be installed.

External window frames had to be painted after a number of years. Classrooms were vacated to allow the painters to do their work. When they were brought into use again it was often found that the windows wouldn't open. This was the cause of the problem in the staff room during the fire.

In 1974 a new county, Cleveland, was formed. It included all of Teesside plus Stockton and Hartlepool. This meant more changes, new Chief Education Officer and other personnel. In later years

ALIAS CHARLIE

the large Cleveland County was dismantled and new authorities were established. Each of these changes were expensive and left Redcar as one of the highest rated areas in the country with less facilities. Pupils no longer go to swimming lessons, the baths have been demolished. Branch libraries are being closed. We keep paying more and getting less.

The school playing fields tended to flood so we had to have sections mole drained.

For many years when the money collected for school dinners was totalled up, a security firm came to collect the cash. It was decided that this was too expensive so the school secretary had to take the money to the local bank and usually I had to run her there in my car and act as security guard.

When I look back I am surprised to find how little attention to the safety of pupils was given by our so called education experts. In my 37 years as a teacher I can recall only one visit from a health and safety inspector and that was in the early years at Nunthorpe. He came, not to check on the situation of pupils and staff but only that of the school secretary. Was there an adult toilet she could use? Could she wash her hands? Was there a health and safety notice displayed in her office?

On wet dinner times pupils are confined in narrow corridors. Have none of our gurus heard of panic escapes?

Some schools are so well protected against people getting into the building that insufficient consideration is given to means of escape.

I always used to tell my pupils about the time when there was a Saturday morning show in a cinema in Paisley. In the projection room a piece of film caught fire. There was no danger to the audience but somebody shouted fire and the children rushed to get out of the main door. In the panic that followed some children were knocked over and trampled to death.

A similar happening took place one Sunday morning at St. James Park, Newcastle. Hundreds of young people had come into the ground to take part in a charity fun walk. People at the back thought the walk had started. They pushed forward and again young people were trampled to death.

We have seen examples of football supporters being killed at Ibrox Park, Glasgow and Hillsborough, Sheffield by people pushing.

In a school of 1,000 pupils it is a rare day when no one starts to feel ill. Who is supposed to look after them? In my day it was often the school secretary who would give a paracetamol tablet to a girl and leave her in the little medical room until a parent could be contacted. Some afternoons there would be three or four girls in the little room. I believe that nowadays pupils must not be given any tablets as some may suffer a reaction.

Pupils, particularly boys, suffered injuries playing games. The injuries might require the attention of a doctor which meant that someone would have to take the pupil to the casualty department of the hospital until a parent arrived to take over.

Things might be better arranged nowadays but then teachers are now so busy doing so much unnecessary paper work which is supposed to check that pupils are achieving standards, often standards which show only the pupil's ability to memorise trivia and are not a real test of ability to think things out. The object seems to be to produce a race of cloned young people who all think alike.

I despair. No matter how hard teachers try the politicians of all parties will mess things up. There are many things that had to be put right but the introduction of league tables only worsens the situation.

It seems that we are no longer thinking about educating chlidren but about promotion and relegation. God help us.

Chapter 38

HILDA

When I was ill Hilda looked after me and the children. She was magnificent in her support. Throughout our life together we were complementary. She was practical. I was a dreamer. She had the push and most times I was happy to be led. We did, of course, argue but usually we made it up in bed.

In 1973 when Margaret had gone off to college, Hilda saw a notice in the local paper asking for volunteers to train to become workers with the Citizen's Advice Bureau (CAB). She applied with a few other ladies and was accepted as a voluntary worker. They attended lectures and courses, sometimes going for a weekend to a university. Hilda made many good friends in the CAB. She usually went on two afternoons per week. She enjoyed the work and I know that the advice she gave was much appreciated. I remember a young baker bringing her two newly baked loaves.

Because of her interests in Arts and Crafts she was invited to become a judge at Castleton Show then also at Danby Show. Later she joined her great friend Betty Groves helping at Hutton Rudby Show. She and Betty used to spend Wednesdays visiting Northallerton. The market was the big attraction to them both. They would have lunch in Osmotherly before returning to Hutton Rudby. I remember travelling home from school on the Parkway when a car overtook me at speed. I thought, I recognise that car then realised it was Hilda trying to get home before me so that she could get the tea ready.

We never got round to having holidays abroad. However, we did get to know North Yorkshire well. In summer, on most Saturdays, we would have a picnic lunch. We kept finding new places where we could picnic in private. I remember picnicking near a little stream and watching a kingfisher diving down to catch little fish.

In the summer of 1983, Hilda and I went to Exeter University for a week's holiday. The previous summer we had gone to Bristol University. We enjoyed these holidays. You slept in rooms used by students in term times. Breakfast and an evening meal were provided so we were able to drive out each day to visit many places we hadn't seen before.

One day at Exeter, Hilda went into the open air swimming pool. Shortly afterwards it seemed to me that she wasn't quite well. When we got home she saw her doctor and then a specialist. They weren't quite sure why she was ill. A year later it was decided that she'd had a mild stroke. Hilda had to give up her work at the CAB.

I thought about retiring but decided to wait till Easter 1984 and retire a month before my 65th birthday.

In the summer of 1985 we heard a radio programme in which it was suggested that mercury amalgam fillings were reputed to be releasing mercury into the bloodstream causing people to be ill. Hilda had all her teeth but she had many mercury amalgam fillings. In the programme it was said that replacing those fillings with a new type of non metallic filling brought about a great improvement in health. The address of a specialist in Harley Streeet who was dealing with this problem was given. I wrote to him and an appointment was made for Hilda to see him. We went down to London, to Harley Street. This specialist carried out some electrical tests and came to the conclusion that she was indeed suffering from mercury poisoning and recommended that she had all her metal fillings replaced.

When we went to see Hilda's dentist in Redcar he would have nothing to do with the idea. I decided to contact the Dental College at Newcastle University. It was the summer holidays but I did speak to the physicist there, who thought there might be something in the idea. He took Hilda's name and address. Later we received a letter saying that the university wanted to carry out a study to see if there was any truth in the idea. If Hilda was willing to be a

ALIAS CHARLIE

volunteer they would arrange to have all her fillings replaced. We went up to see the professor and his No. 2 where the matter was discussed and I outlined Hilda's recent health record.

We started to go regularly to see Mr Cassidy the Senior Registrar in Restorative Dentistry. He was meticulous in his work. He took great care to see that all the amalgam was being sucked up by a little vacuum cleaner as it was being removed from the tooth. This carried on for several weeks and when all the work had been completed it was arranged that we would return to see him in three month's time. At first I felt that the treatment had improved Hilda but it became apparent that she was no better. We went back again after six months. None of the volunteers had improved as a result of the treatment and the trial was ended.

Hilda's health started to deteriorate. She hadn't the energy she used to have. Her speech was becoming blurred. In 1986 Hilda had another stroke then in 1989 she had a heart attack and was taken into South Cleveland Hospital for intensive care. In 1992 she had a severe stroke which paralysed her left side for a while and left her with difficulties in swallowing and in breathing. The doctor wanted her to go into hospital but Hilda didn't want to go so I said I'd look after her. She was referred to the outpatients department for the Elderly where she was examined. She then went on a course of speech therapy but it wasn't very successful. We went to Middlesbrough once a week for an hour. She was asked to read aloud but quickly she became confused and her speech became slurred.

Meanwhile I had been ill with severe breathing problems and I also had a hernia. I spent two nights in Stead Hospital using oxygen. An appointment was made for me to see a specialist in six week's time. I didn't think I'd last that long so I went private. I was seen at the Nuffield Hospital and an X ray was taken. It was then arranged that I should go to South Cleveland Hospital where I had blood tests, an ECG, and echo sounding. Dr Hall prescribed Lisinopril and Warfarin in addition to the Digoxin I'd been taking for many years. As I started to improve Dr Hall recommended that I have my hernia operation which I had in October 1993.

Whilst I was out of action the family rallied round and looked after Hilda.

In October 1997 Hilda was back in the Coronary Care Unit suffering from a silent heart attack and renal failure. She was not expected to survive but she did and came home two weeks later.

In January 1998 Hilda was back in South Cleveland Hospital suffering from anaemia. She was given a blood transfusion but unfortunately in her sleep she pulled out the tube attached to the needle and didn't get the full transfusion.

She was back in again in February for another transfusion. On 26th February I brought her back home. As she got out of the car she stumbled and gashed her leg on the edge of the concrete drive. I phoned for an ambulance but we had to wait more that two hours before one was available. She was taken to Middlesbrough General Hospital where her wounds were eventually stitched up at 11 p.m. She came home the next day and her doctor arranged for a wheelchair and oxygen cylinders to be supplied. She was now incontinent and needing constant care. Most days a nurse would come in to dress her wounds. Twice a week a bath nurse would come to give her a good wash down. I had two beds brought down into the dining room since she couldn't climb the stairs.

It was becoming increasingly difficult to feed her and to make sure she swallowed her tablets. In August she had to go back to intensive care in South Cleveland Hospital. She had been having a number of strokes and her consultant told me her brain had been destroyed. She was no longer able to swallow and had to be fed through a tube into her stomach. After weeks she was sent to the Stead Hospital in Redcar where she was really well looked after, until she died ten weeks later on 24th November 1998.

It is difficult to come to terms with this. She was a fighter and put up a very brave fight right up to the end. I could not have had a better wife and she was a superb mother and grandmother.

Chapter 39

I'm an old man. Looking back on my life I've been extremely fortunate. Hilda and I were together for 57 years. My family is very supportive and my grandchildren are sensible and hardworking.

Each generation hopes that it will set a good example for the future and make life better for their successors. Here doubts start to creep in.

How many teachers stay on till they are 65 as I did? Why are there so few?

My suspicion is that they have felt undervalued. They have been messed about so much by politicians. OFSTED is getting a reputation like the secret police. Your best is never quite good enough.

Useless paper work is harming schools, hospitals, farming and industry.

How are we going to survive in the future? We have shut almost all the coal mines. Steel works are fast disappearing. Shipbuilding has gone. Manufacturers of clothing are being replaced by cheap imports from abroad. Motor car manufacturing is fast disappearing. To sell a pig, sheep or cow in the market you have to list its pedigree, fill up forms then be lucky to be able to pay the auctioneer from the proceeds of the sale. Many of the big grain farmers can make more profit from letting their fields go back to nature rather than growing crops.

Railway transport is in a mess. The train arriving at Euston is 20 minutes late. Tomorrow it will be back to normal, 30 minutes late.

Villages are losing their banks and post offices. Soon it will only be the wealthy who can afford to live in the country.

How do we survive in a country that produces so little. Well, we manage to sell arms to many countries which are divided by race and religion. Many third world countries struggle like mad to pay the interest on debts owed to us.

We are over governed. There are now so many institutions at different levels which control our lives. Each is feathering its own nest.

I remember too clearly the Wall Street crash and the years of the depression. If anyone has not seen the film or read the book,'The Grapes of Wrath' by John Steinbeck, I'd advise them to get a copy.

Some day our young people will realise that 'the Emperor is wearing no clothes'. I hope the revolution is not too violent.

To me the great explosion of money into the Internet is certain to cause financial chaos. I see it as being like the South Sea Bubble of 1720 and the Wall Street crash of 1929.

More and more the familiar names of British companies are disappearing as they become parts of multi-national firms who are happy to transfer production of goods to wherever it can be done most cheaply.

We are helpless in the hands of the accountants, lawyers and politicians.

Does history repeat itself? I think it does but in different ways.

My one consolation is that I have, in the past, been so wrong in my predictions that this scenario is unlikely to happen. There may be a young Bill Gates somewhere who will see that surplus food from the rich countries can go to those who are starving in other parts of the world and be able to arrange this without upsetting the world economy.

Whenever there is a major disaster there are millions of people world wide who do their best to mitigate the effects by giving money, time and goods to help out. Surely all these good people will be able to have some influence on the future.

Problems will always arise and solutions need to be found. The world is constantly changing. After each Winter comes the Spring. New life appears to brighten up our daily lives. Just to sit in the sunlight makes us feel so much better.

We cannot afford to ignore what is happening but so long as we know the problems we can start to work on the solutions.

I wish I was young again to take up the challenge.